9780836952001

THE ELDER HENRY JAMES
(1811–1882)

HENRY JAMES
1811-1882

AUSTIN WARREN

THE ELDER
HENRY JAMES

BOOKS FOR LIBRARIES PRESS
FREEPORT, NEW YORK

First Published 1934
Reprinted 1970

STANDARD BOOK NUMBER:
8369-5200-6

LIBRARY OF CONGRESS CATALOG CARD NUMBER:
75-107835

PRINTED IN THE UNITED STATES OF AMERICA

To

E. A. W. and L. F. H.

IN GRATITUDE AND AFFECTION

PREFACE

MORE than ten years ago my attention was first called
to the elder Henry James. The introduction I owe to
my friend, Dr Clarence Hotson. This book has been
five years in the making, but was virtually complete two
years ago, before the appearance of Mr Grattan's *Three
Jameses* called the attention of literary folk to the distinguished father of two distinguished sons. During
the fifty years since his death, however, the subject of
this volume has never wanted intelligent and zealous
disciples or praise, albeit the disciples have been few and
scattered, and the praise, though discerning, incidental
to the celebration of one or the other of the sons. The
time now seems ripe for James to receive attention in
his own right, both as personality and as thinker.

In this book I have been chiefly concerned with pre-
senting James, in his own characteristic language; with
tracing his philosophical development against the back-
ground of what is to me the most exciting period in our

intellectual history—the twenty or thirty years preceding the Civil War; and with interpreting his by no means pellucid, often baffling, but always stimulating books. My attitude might be described as in the main that of sympathetic detachment. In the Epilogue, I have brought James out of his own time and into ours, and have asked (and tried to answer) the questions, What part would he play in the current scene; what cause would he espouse; and, finally, what can be urged in behalf of his central attitude? But nowhere should I be understood as speaking my own convictions upon the doctrines James enounced or the position which he adopted toward the issues of his day and ours. I explore; I interpret; I do not pass judgment. But my former teacher, Irving Babbitt, whose death cannot terminate his constant inspiration of those whose minds he awakened, would visit me with proper scorn if I allowed myself to feel that the detachment of the chronicler or the sympathetic interpretation (*e.g.*, trying to see the world from inside Henry James) were the whole duty of the writing man. In a subsequent volume, *The Age of Emerson,* I hope to give a considered estimate of the cause James served—in other words, to speak as a critic.

An apology is due the *manes* of the unpedantic seer for the documentation of this book. But, relegated to the back of the text, it need disturb no reader who would dispense with it. Because, however, the elder James scattered his brilliant *aperçus* so indiscriminately through the whole range of his books, tracts, articles,

reviews, and letters, and because he runs the gamut of
his favorite themes in well-nigh every published appearance, it is doubtful that any memory can recall
where to locate a particular utterance. I cannot pretend to offer a complete repertory of the wit and wisdom of Henry James; but I am inclined to agree with
his son William that a collection of his best passages
would do him more service than the republication of
any single work, and the notes and index to this book
will make accessible those of the 'best passages' which
I have incorporated into this *l'homme et l'œuvre.*

Throughout my study, I have had the cordial assistance of Mr Henry James of New York, able con-
tinuator of the family tradition; Professor Ralph Barton
Perry of Harvard, literary executor of the James manuscripts, who has permitted me full access to the letters
and papers in the Widener Library; Professor Harold
A. Larrabee of Union College, to whose interest we
owe much of the new information concerning William
James of Albany; and Mr Samuel C. Eby of New
York, lifelong student of the elder James' philosophy.
All four of these gentlemen have read the manuscript
of this book, and I am deeply indebted to them for
their strictures and suggestions. To Mr James' kindness, I owe the permission to reproduce Duveneck's
portrait as frontispiece.

The assistance and encouragement given me by
descendants of James and his friend, Garth Wilkinson,
by American and English students of James and his
philosophy, and by my New-Church friends have been

most heartening. I would particularly mention Miss
Charlotte Schetter, Mrs L. C. Jervis, Mrs Alice Spiers
Sechrist, Mrs George Vaux, Mrs Mary Wilkinson
Matthews, Miss Florence Pertz, the Revd. Lewis Field
Hite, Mr B. A. Whittemore, Mr Hartley Grattan,
Mr Hansell Baugh, and the officials of the Swedenborg
House, London.

A part of this book was written during my year as
Fellow of the American Council of Learned Societies,
and to the Council I extend my gratitude for the opportunities it afforded me.

To my colleague and friend, Professor Irving H.
White, I am indebted for kind assistance in reading
proof.

A. W.

Boston University,
6 February 1934.

CONTENTS

PROLOGUE

THERE are many things which money may beget: more money, for example, or idle dissipation, or leisure for art and reflection. High amongst the many distinctions of the James family must be set the admirable uses to which they devoted the wealth inherited from their shrewd progenitor, William of Albany. They became philosophers, painters, writers, gentlemen of cultivated and speculative tastes. Wealth, as well as breeding, has its obligations. Those who are freed, whether by abundance of means or paucity of wants, from daily labor for daily bread may, by a little effort, enjoy a detachment difficult for the majority of men. Of course there is an inhuman sort of insulation, a temperamental or reasoned frigidity which may well be the unpardonable sin. But there is possible also an intellectual detachment quite compatible with the warmest sensibility to the needs of one's fellows and the most ardent purpose of assisting them to achieve the abundant life not now theirs.

The elder Henry James, financially independent at twenty-one, turned his freedom to the pursuit of philosophy. Endowed with a thirst for truth, he enquired diligently of all the seers and sages in which his day abounded. Sandeman, Fourier, Swedenborg: all these in turn served him as guides in his pilgrimage. But he achieved at length the objective of every philosopher: he formulated the meaning of life for himself. He was not ashamed of his intellectual paternity; and, never coveting the name of 'original,' he would have been content to call his doctrine an interpretation of Swedenborg. But others who proudly claimed the authority of the Swedish seer disavowed James' version; and, since he repudiated their organization and cared nothing for magisterial names, he was content to have it so.

The philosopher worthy of the name assimilates all that kindred minds, past and present, can offer him, and then effects, through the medium of his own temperament, a synthesis. This James did. He fused his reading and experience and thought, and he transferred his matured vision to paper in a richly personal idiom.

Were the times propitious for his full intellectual development? No—and yes. His son William thought his father born too late; conjectured that he might have played a really momentous part had he emerged upon some vigorously theological age when the best minds concerned themselves with nice and vehemently urged definitions of Divinity. And certainly James

spoke the language of metaphysical theology in a day
when there were few who uttered or comprehended it.
But, since it was a social gospel to which James ap-
propriated his language, it might, with equal plausibil-
ity, be asserted that he came too early.

Speculations of this sort never troubled James. He
accepted time and place as appointed. And it is by no
means certain that, with his *liaison* of theological and
social aptitudes, he was not justified. His intellectual
development fell within a rich and exhilarating, if
incautious, period: that of the eighteen forties and
fifties, the era of reformist zeal and Transcendentalist
speculation to which the Civil War wrote an approxi-
mate *finis*. Those were days when intellectuals cherished high hopes for the universe and possessed confidence in the power of reason and good will to effect
its salvation. Their hopes proved premature; yet one
cannot but envy the credulity with its consequent
impetus to thought and action.

James was not a New Englander and not a Transcendentalist: he ever tempered his idealism with the
good sense of the cosmopolitan. But he owed much
to his time. There was open vision in those days; and
if, as it happened, his message received less attention
than that of many rival preachers, he had the comfort
of living in a prophetic era.

His faith sustained him. Though he was uncommonly blessed in his marriage and his children, he
lived by his word and for its delivery.

His independence, wit, and piquant idiom served

to make him a subject for anecdotes. His relations
as friend and father introduce persons, and those celebrated, into his chronicle. But events, sayings, and
personalities must yield to the development of a doctrine. James' biography is properly and primarily
that of a mind.

THE ELDER HENRY JAMES

CHAPTER I

FAMILY AND COLLEGE

▄▄

I

THE James family made their home in a comfortable brick house on North Pearl Street in Albany; and, besides the surviving progeny of three marriages—to the number of eleven—the household frequently included visiting clergymen of the Presbyterian faith. Living was on a bountiful scale; and this note of bounty, of liberality, of expansiveness, was to characterize successive generations of the family.

The head of the Albany household was called William James. Irish born, he journeyed to America at the age of eighteen: the traditional story has it that he landed in the poverty and obscurity appropriate to a potential merchant prince, his sole possessions 'a little money, a Latin grammar . . . and a great desire to visit one of the Revolutionary battlefields.'[1]

There is, however, a rival, and less romantic, version. According to this, James' father preceded him to this country, the son following some time later, only to be sent back to Ireland to settle an estate. Having discharged this responsibility, he took the liberty to invest the proceeds in English merchandise, which he shipped to America and sold. In consequence, after paying his father the money due him, he had left to himself a liberal amount with which to inaugurate his own career.[2]

In 1793 William James reached Albany; and the rest of his life comprises the history of ever expanding commercial enterprise. For two years he served as clerk. Then, with the aid of a partner, he set up business as a tobacconist. Two years later, he added a shop for the marketing of farmers' produce and dry goods; yet a year later, he erected a tobacco factory. He operated an express business between Albany and Utica. He leased and managed the salt works of Syracuse. He bought land in Albany, Utica, Syracuse, and New York City.

Honors and responsibilities appropriately befell him. Streets in Albany and Syracuse and a village in New York State derived their names from him. In Albany, his power and reputation found superiors only in those of the last patroon, Stephen Van Rensselaer. James helped to organize the Savings Bank and the Chamber of Commerce, serving as first vice-president of both. Two years after its establishment in 1813, he was made a trustee of Albany Academy, and subsequently, from 1826 on, he was chairman of the board. The First Presbyterian Church made him a trustee in 1820; and Union College (presided over by a former pastor of First Church) assigned him the same distinction in 1832.[3]

From the inception of the project, James had been interested in the Erie Canal; he had defended the digging of "that ditch" when conservative men shook their heads with prudent dubiety. In return for this faith, he headed the Citizens' Committee of Albany on Nov. 2, 1825, at the celebration which attended the inauguration of the Canal. His devotion to the cause found fitting recognition in his selection as orator of the day. With natural satisfaction he hailed American industry and ingenuity, American achievement and prosperity, and found, in all this, testimony that a discerning Heaven had judged the new nation a people to be especially watched and favored.[4]

This great inaugurator of a great family died in 1832, leaving an estate estimated at three million. The end of his career came at its height: the Albany *Evening Journal* proclaimed his death 'a severe loss to the city of Albany. He had done more to build up the city than any other individual.'[5]

His will, a lengthy and elaborate document indeed, was broken in court; but it was printed in full and yet bears testimony to the sober sense of its testator. It premissed that 'in view . . . of the lamentable consequences which so frequently result to young persons brought up in affluence from coming at once into the possession of property,' the final settlement of the estate should not be made 'until the youngest of my children and grandchildren living at the date of this my will and attaining the age of twenty-one years shall have attained that age.' That his descendants should constitute one of the few patrician families of the country seems not to have been the founder's design. His American belief in the dignity of labor emerges squarely in the proposition that in order to have the benefit of his provisions three of his sons and a grandson 'must severally learn some one of the professions, trades or occupations usually pursued in this country as a livelihood, and must assiduously pursue and practise the same.'[6]

William James was thrice married. The first wife brought him twin sons, dying eight days after the gift. The second, by whom he had a daughter, died less than two years after the marriage. The third, Catharine Barber, bore him seven sons and three daughters and survived her husband some twenty-seven years.[7]

Of stock originally Scotch-Irish, the third Mrs James could boast a creditable American pedigree: her grandfather was a judge, her father and two uncles were officers in the Revolutionary War, and they possessed other claims to attention and respect.[8] But Catharine James held herself not at all high. Her fourth son, Henry, testified of her, with delicious deprecation, 'my mother was a good wife and mother, nothing else,— save, to be sure, a kindly friend and neighbor.' She plumed herself not at all upon her illustrious uncles, the friends of Lafayette and Washington, for tales of whom her children begged her; she seemed to take

pleasure in chatting with the women who came in to
sew for her; while a woman of dignity and position,
she lacked any touch of the snob. It was she who dispensed to the needy poor the stock of beef and pork
and potatoes which her husband laid by for the purpose
at the beginning of each winter. Her sons and daughters—not only her own eight, but her three step-
children—felt for her admiration as well as affection.'

A grandmother there was too in the house, who
loved and interested the children. Brought up in the
logic of Calvin and of an impeccably devout temperament, she came, as she grew older, to doubt whether
this dogmatic theology could truly represent the Christian religion; and 'the conflict grew so active erelong
between this quickened allegiance of her heart to God
and the merely habitual deference her intellect was
under to men's opinions, as to allow her afterwards
no fixed rest this side of the grave.' Finding no mental
security, she turned from her head to her heart, and
from the Law to the Gospel. She lived in her affections; and there was a winsome spontaneity in her
goodness which her grandchildren always remembered.[10]

II

The family formed a self-contained, self-sufficient
unit, presided over by its patriarchal head. Was this
not indeed the customary unit of nineteenth-century
society? Son Henry, who longed for himself and all
men to be lovers of the whole human race, could, look-

ing back at the end of his life upon the *home* of his youth, discern in its domestic version of Christianity no difference from that of its neighbors. 'Contented isolation' struck him as the vice common to all. Like all the other families of the land, his own 'gave no sign of a *spontaneous* religious culture, or of affections touched to the dimensions of universal man.'[11] *Being good* consisted of attending family prayers and loving one's relatives and bestowing charity upon the needy poor about one.

Nor had the form of religion in which Henry was reared that emotional impetus, that self-forgetting abandonment to the cause of the world's redemption, which a boy requires to fire him. Even the Presbyterian clergy, who were familiar intimates of the James house, led him, by neither their manners nor conversation, to suppose that religion was more than a 'higher prudence, or that there was anything whatever in the Divine character as revealed in the gospel of Christ to inflame in common minds an enthusiasm of devotion, or beget anything like a passionate ardor of self-abasement.'[12]

This decorous and safe religion offered little to stir the imagination of the young or quicken in them the impulse to high deed and self-forgetful purpose. Saving one's soul involved a kind of documented and charted traffic with the Deity, the proper procedure for which was to be found in the Bible. Heaven was the reward for obeying the rules, and Hell the awful penalty for refusing the minimum of homage.

The God of this desiccating religion was a being beyond the comprehension of children and even men: as Arnold used to put it, *a magnified and non-natural man*.[13] This magnified and non-natural man bore a persistent resentment against mankind because, as one was taught, all mankind had 'originally forfeited the creative good-will in the person of Adam, their attorney or representative'; so that every man comes into the world a sinner from his mother's womb, redeemable not by any conceivable or achievable merit of his own, but solely through the blood of Christ shed for an Atonement.[14]

Was one saved or no? Was one sure that he was approved by this inexorable Deity,—blameless in His sight. In ages of fervent devotion and intense, consuming piety, Christians had returned to a belief that only faith could justify: humanity could not by its virtue find acceptance with Heaven: even the saint was 'all unrighteousness.' But this humility disappears when piety waxes cold. In the boyhood of Henry James, Protestants continued to profess that all men were of themselves and in themselves equally under the Divine censure; but they really believed that good works entitled one to salvation; that God loved the saint and hated the sinner.

Such a theology of moral distinctions induced, in the young Henry James, a morbid preoccupation with the state of his own soul. 'My boyish animal spirits,' he writes, 'allowed me no doubt very little time for reflection; yet it was very seldom that I lay down at night without a present thought of God, and some little effort of recoil upon myself. . . .; the dark silent night usually led in the spectral eye of God, and set me to wondering and pondering evermore how I should effectually baffle its gaze.' [15] His conscience occupied itself in keeping a 'debtor and creditor account with God,' now flattering itself with Pharisaic self-approval of its purity, now despairing of itself as utterly loathsome in the Divine eye.

The Lord's especial Day seemed particularly designed to torment children: 'we were taught not to play, not to dance, nor to sing, not to read story-books, not to con over our school-lessons for Monday even; not to whistle, not to ride the pony, nor to take a walk in the country, nor a swim in the river; nor, in short, to do anything which nature specially craved.' The day abounded in prohibitions difficult of children's observance; and 'nothing is so hard for a child as not-to-do.' [16]

III

Henry James early came to feel that his nature craved a larger conception of the Divine than was mediated through church and family. Even when he suffered from conscience and lay awake in bed, encompassed with the terrors of hell, he was moved not by 'any technical offense which I had committed against established decorum, but always [by] some wanton ungenerous word or deed by which I had wounded the vital self-respect of another. . . . I sometimes wantonly mocked the sister who was nearest me in age, and now and then violently repelled the overtures of a younger brother who aspired to associate himself with me in my sports and pastimes.' These defects of tenderness and sympathy, rather than his 'original sin' as a descendant of the ancestral Adam, moved the boy's heart to contrition.[17]

His affections overflowed the bounds of the family and the clan. In retrospect he could write: 'even in infancy the family subject feels an instinct of opposition to domestic rule. Even as a child he feels the family bond irksome, and finds his most precious enjoyments and friendships outside the home precinct.' Henry 'was never so happy at home as away from it. And even within the walls of home my happiest moments were those spent in the stable talking horse-talk with Asher Foot, the family coachman; in the wood-house talking pigeons, chickens, and rabbits with Francis Piles, the out-door servant; in the kitchen, in the evenings, hearing Dinah Foot the cook, and Peter Woods the waiter, discourse of rheumatism, method-ism, and miracle, with a picturesque good faith, super-stition, and suavity that made the parlor converse insipid; or, finally, in the bedrooms teasing the good-natured chambermaids till their rage died out in convulsions of impotent laughter, and they threatened the next time they caught me to kiss me till my cheeks burnt crimson.'[18]

A shoemaker's shop in the neighborhood offered a favorite refuge from too constraining a domesticity.

The business was operated by two young fellows, 'uncommonly bright, intelligent, and personable,' who impressed their juniors as abounding in knowledge of the world. The boys of the neighborhood congregated there to indulge in games, conversation, and clandestine feasts provided from their family larders. In his friends, the shoemakers, Henry James found a freedom from Presbyterian decorum which struck him as altogether delightful. 'They had, to begin with, such an immense force of animal spirits as magnetised one out of all self-distrust or timidity, barely to be with them. And then they were so utterly void of all religious sensibility or perturbation that my moral sinews relaxed at once into comparative ease and freedom. . . .' The young artisans read with avidity what books their well-to-do patrons lent them; they were constant in their patronage of such theatrical performances as the amateur company of the city produced, and eagerly criticized the acting; they had a fancy for oratory and patriotic eloquence. Into the shop Henry brought collections of speeches from the James library, and read aloud by the hour. 'There was an old workman in the shop, an uncle of the principals, who sacrificed occasionally to Bacchus, and whose eyes used to drip very freely when I read Robert Emmet's famous speech, or the plea of the prisoner's counsel at the trial scene in "The Heart of Midlothian".'[19]

Henry needed no supernatural Absolute to stimulate his curiosity or quicken his appetite for existence. His youth fathered his maturity in its unconquerable joy

of living. 'I had always had,' he writes of his childhood, 'the keenest savor and relish of whatsoever came
to me by nature's frank inspiration or free gift. The
common ore of existence perpetually converted itself
into the gold of life in the glowing fire of my animal
spirits. I lived in every fibre of my body. The dawn
always found me on my feet; and I can still vividly
recall the divine rapture which filled my blood as
I pursued under the magical light of morning the
sports of the river, the wood, or the field.' [20]

IV

At the age of thirteen the boy met with an accident
so serious as to have maimed the spirit of any less
valiant soul. A schoolboy at the Albany Academy,
then comprising four teachers and some hundred and
thirty students, he was one of a group who met in
the park in the front of the Academy for experiments,
at once instructive and amusing, in balloon flying. A
ball of tow soaked in turpentine furnished the motive
power. When the balloon caught fire, the ball would
drop, to be kicked about by the boys. On the occasion
of one such pastime, when Henry had acquired a
sprinkling of turpentine on his pantaloons, one of
the balls was sent flying through the open window
of a stable. The boy, intent only upon putting out
the fire, rushed to the hayloft and stamped out the
flame. But in so doing, he burned his leg. The consequence was a confinement to his bed for the next two

years, and the double amputation of one leg above the knee.[21]

Henry did not return to the Academy after his accident, but prepared for college with the assistance of a tutor. In 1828, at the age of seventeen, he entered Union College, Schenectady, as a member of the Junior Class, making his home in the household of Dr Nott.[22]

V

Dr Eliphalet Nott, Union's most distinguished President, was then in the midst of his sixty-two years reign, which lasted from 1804 until his death in 1866.[23] Between him and the wealthy merchant, William James of Albany, there must long have existed relations of friendship and respect, for, before going to Schenectady, Dr Nott occupied, from 1798 on, the pulpit of the First Presbyterian Church of Albany, where, in company with the other citizens of Scotch-Irish origin, Mr James discharged his Sabbath duty to the Deity.[24]

From 1821 to 1826, the relations of President and Merchant were especially and strikingly close. Nott, a man of intrepid courage and determination, supported his college and raised endowment by any means that came to hand. In 1805, he lobbied the State Legislature into giving him $80,000 in the form of a lottery grant; in 1814, he secured from the same authority a similar grant of $200,000. The second lottery fared ill: in desperation, Nott borrowed from James, giving as security bonds owned by the College. This was the first of a series of such loans. By 1823, James had in his possession, as pledge for Nott's indebtedness, the deed to '67 acres near Troy turnpike; also the New College Edifices and all the houses standing on the premises.' In 1826, James advanced $100,000 for paying off lottery prizes. The following year, he was made Trustee of Union and a member of its finance committee. When the Trustee died, in 1832, he left the College a box full of cancelled checques and released securities.[25]

Dr Nott's audacity extended beyond finance. His judgment of men and his views of religion and life shrewdly transcended his clerical garb and denominational tenets. Of his own profession, he admitted: 'Ministers, as a class, know less practically of human nature than any other class of men. . . . [; they] ordinarily see only the brighter side of the world. Almost everybody treats them with civility, the religious with peculiar kindness and attention.' Contrasting them with the lawyers, who see the worst side of the world, he berated the clergy for their inefficiency, their lack of 'directness of appeal. They want the same go-ahead, common-sense way of interesting men lawyers have.'

He confessed himself 'disgusted and grieved with the religious controversies of the present age. The divisions of schools, old schools and new schools, and the polemical fury with which the contest is waged, are entirely foreign to the true spirit of Christianity.' Even Rome came within the limits of his toleration:

'there is a great deal of religion in that church;' while he did not hesitate to say that Luther's character was, in some of its features, 'harsh, rugged, and unlovely.'

To the sceptics among his students, this outspoken President did not hesitate to confess that, during the French Revolution, he had been 'troubled with the same difficulties.' [26]

In Nott's time, the college curriculum consisted principally of the classics and mathematics, with some tincture of rhetoric and natural science. [27] During his junior year Henry James pursued studies in Horace, Cicero, selected Greek authors—apparently including Sophocles and Euripides, conic sections, political economy, and natural philosophy. The records of his senior course are less complete, but they include work in Biot's Optics and Kames' *Elements of Criticism*. [28] Dr Nott himself took the class in Kames, and made it more of a Socratic dialogue than either lecture or recitation. Some topic being suggested by the chapter on physics, or morals, or political economy, each of the students would be drawn to define his views, and those views would be analysed and developed by the instructor in such a way as to clarify all the issues that had been raised. [29] Dr Nott's genuine liberalism involved an effort to lead his students to think for themselves and to distrust mere authoritarian pronouncements; in consequence of which those of his pupils who achieved for themselves intellectual careers were found entertaining all the varieties of religious

and metaphysical opinion. Romanists, High and Low
Anglicans, Calvinists, Baptists, as well as such doughty
independents as Henry James, were all characteristic
products of Dr Nott's tutelage.[30]

James doubtless derived far more intellectual stim-
ulus from his course in Kames than from his study of
'Intellectual Philosophy,' in which the text appears
to have been the standard *'Locke on the Understanding.'* James was all his life rather impatient of technical metaphysics; and, too, his mind and temperament were quite as averse to any sort of empiricism
as those of his friend Emerson.[31]

Himself reared in the most rigid of Presbyterianism, James must have felt in the warmest sympathy
with Dr Nott's theological and ecclesiastical liberalism.
Nott was a man of pragmatic interests, who laid more
stress on character than creed. Innocent of a speculative turn of mind, he appears never to have rejected the
theology of the Westminster Catechism in which he
had been reared; but his doctrine was neither Edward-
sean, nor Hopkinsian, nor Emmonsian. He had no
desire to fathom the inscrutable decrees of the Almighty, and felt no impulse to push beyond such
revelation as had been vouchsafed in Scripture. With
cordial good will he preached in churches of all the
evangelical faiths; and he could not be induced to
manifest quite the proper degree of alarm at the rise
of the Unitarian movement in New England.[32]

As befitted a person of so mild and rational a temper, Dr Nott was little inclined to the popular revival

movements of his day, which stirred minds like Henry James with such revulsion. Officially supporting such as came within his jurisdiction, he was always suspected by the more elect among his students of some lukewarmness in his character as a religionist, some latitudinarian laxness.[33]

In fine, Dr Nott's influence must have been the most telling that was brought to bear upon James in his student days, and surely one of the principal forces concurring to foster his own liberalism.

James' grades placed him in the first third of his class, just short of Phi Beta Kappa. His physical disability did not have the effect of driving him into absorption with his books any more than it hindered his participation in social life. More than from the formal courses of the college he probably profited from his close association, as member of the recently formed Sigma Phi Fraternity, with the warm-hearted young men whose 'brother' he became.[34]

VI

His life at Union was interrupted in mid-course by the dramatic flight to Boston, which, as *Notes of a Son* hints,[35] was the consequence of a clash of wills between Henry and his father. The 'clash' arose from Henry's disinclination to study law and his practise of giving, in payment for the luxuries which he relished—good cigars, oysters, smart tailoring, books —drafts upon the credit of his opulent sire.

The elder James was much alarmed at these evidences of worldliness—and worse—in his son; and bestirred his friend, the distinguished lawyer, Archibald McIntyre, to write the youth a letter of warning. Under the date of November 12, 1829, McIntyre rebukes the worldling.

'I have heard, and your friends generally have heard enough of your conduct to cause us much pain and solicitude for your safety and future usefulness. I consider you on the very verge of ruin. . . . Allow me then to entreat that you will for the future repose yourself upon your father and mother, and take their advice in everything. Indulge in no expenses whatever that shall not be known to and approved by them. . . . Let your studies too as far as possible be conformable to your father's wishes. You intimated to me that you disliked the law. . . . On speaking to your father on this head, however, I found him inflexibly fixed on your studying the law, or at all events on studying one of the learned professions. . . .

. . . Some consider you already as lost, irretrievably lost. I am not, however, one of those. I cannot believe that a young man of good parts, with wealth to support him in well doing (but with none without performing his duty), with numerous and anxious friends, can be such an idiot as to throw away all these advantages, and become a loathing to himself and his best friends.'

The warning was insufficient, or came too late. By the second of December, when William James irately writes McIntyre, Henry has already left college and fled. He 'has so debased himself as to leave his parents house in the character of a swindler etc. etc.— details presented today—are the order which I enclose as a specimen of his progress in arts of low vileness—and unblushing falsehood;—such will be practised in N.Y.—in book stores—Taylors etc.—and in the same as dfts on me etc.;—all of which will meet him direct—and lodge him in a prison of some kind directly; a fellow from Schenectady was after him today for 50 to 60 drs—(in a note I understand) for segars and oysters. . . . Townsend—Sons—and others from the College have reported through the City—that he is gone to Boston—and I understand he told the man who gave the cloth that he was going there— but deception is of no consequence in his case [36]—they will find him and he will find his reward, poor being. . . .'

No such dire fate as was prophecied befell the culprit. He made his way to Boston, but his stay appears to have been in no sense a rigorous chastisement of his wildness. On January 30, 1830, he addressed to Isaac Jackson, tutor in mathematics at Union and quite evidently Henry's intimate friend into the bargain, a long letter [37] which reveals him as temporarily earning his honest living as a proofreader and meanwhile enjoying, with the gusto persistently his, the pleasures, social and sermonic, of Boston.

'After all the great step has been taken,' he writes, 'and I am alone in my pilgrimage. . . . Here I am in the good town of *Bosting* very comfortably situated on the first floor (not the basement) of a four story house in Hancock Street, occupied by Mr Jenks.[38] The room contains a very valuable and curious library (4 large cases). My bed stands in a neat recess, on either side of which opens a handsome closet. I am sitting on a snug sofa. . . . On my left is a cheerful Lehigh fire; under my feet a warm carpet and over my head a painting of Lorenzo de Medici, by Mrs Jenks. This room is sacred to me.

'Mr Jenks ranks high as a scholar, and is very liberal in encouragement. He will afford me during the first year of my stay about $200 exclusive of my board and lodging in his own family. I am occupied about 8 hours per day, in reading proofs etc. This has been called by Mr McIntyre "drudgery." But it is quite a misnomer. I have to search out every quotation (say in Paley's Nat. Theoly. which Mr J. is now publishing) and ascertain whether it be correct; and if it be not, to amend it. When a short notice may be wanting for the [Christian] Examiner etc I am expected to prepare it. . . . I now go on with the study of languages much more thoroughly than I should have found it necessary had I remained at home. It is indispensable that I should. My ambition is awakened; I have here every advantage, and the least shall not be slighted.'

He finds his evenings occupied to quite as much advantage as his days. 'I have been introduced into some of the first society here, and almost all I know afford me every requisite attention. Mrs Jenks is one

of the most accomplished ladies of the city. Miss J.
her sister in law, is a very amiable sensible young lady,
and withal an enchanting singer. So you see into
what a circle I have been launched!'

His Sundays too offer their opportunities: he has
critically sampled the leading pulpits of the city. 'Mr
Jenks is, you know, a Unitarian, but no way anxious
to direct me in the choice of a preacher. I hear Dr
Channing[39] occasionally and I should never wish a
higher treat than one of his practical sermons. Mr
Potter,[40] however, who has been exceedingly kind to
me, has numbered me amongst his hearers.'

The letter speedily returns, at the mention of the
last name, from clergymen to charming women. 'Mrs
Potter is what Eve might have been before the Fall.
Listening to and looking upon her sometimes, I am
apt . . . to wish with the Psalmist, neither poverty
nor riches, but just such a wife as Mrs Potter; (by
the way, what a horrid name for *that* woman).'

VII

However agreeable the society of Boston, the sojourn with the hospitable Jenks family was merely
episodic in length. The conflict of wills which had
occasioned the exile was in some way terminated, and
the young man returned to Albany, to pass four years,
or thereabouts, in a variety of professional essays.

The chronicle of these years must remain vague;
but we have James' own word that he made an effort

to please his father by studying law.[41] And his name appeared from October 1831 through February of the following year as one of the editors of the Albany *Daily Craftsman,* a four-page sheet issued in opposition to the 'Albany Regency' and in active support of President Jackson.[42]

Two years after Henry's graduation from Union, the redoubtable William James departed this life. In spite of his effort to cut off with small annuities his two theologically minded sons, Henry and William, both of whom he regarded as unsound in the faith, the will was broken, and Henry, along with his brothers, found himself, upon coming of age, 'leisured for life,' and consequently able to work out, as he chose, his cultural and spiritual salvation.

CHAPTER II

SEMINARY AND SANDEMAN

··

I

HENRY JAMES' deeply religious nature at length suggested the ministry as a suitable profession; and Dr
Nott's liberalism must have intimated the possibility
of finding a vocation in the church without too much
sacrifice of charity to doctrinal correctness. For one
reared in the Presbyterian sect, Princeton was the
natural theological seminary to choose; and Henry's
half-brother William [1] had studied there from 1816
to 1819, prior to his ordination. Henry entered with
the class of 1835, which comprised fifty-eight men; [2]
and he remained for two years and a half.

Dr Archibald Alexander then presided over the
Seminary; and its faculty yet harbored the celebrated
Dr Charles Hodge, who once boasted that he had
taught theology fifty years without ever introducing
a new idea. The professors gave James ready access to
their houses and their conversation, and exposed him
to the full logic of high Calvinism; but James grew

restless and interrogative. The arbitrary despotism attributed to the Deity made him shudder; nor could Dr Alexander explain the doctrine of justification by faith to his satisfaction. 'Don't you see?' constantly iterated the good doctor. James did not, and could not pretend that he did. Faith surely cannot be limited to anything so meager as intellectual assent to a doctrine or proposition; surely it must lay hold upon the heart, upon life. Even the devils *believe* and tremble. The Princeton professors referred James' opinion to Satan. But he met with great favor in the social life of the seminary; and at least one of his professors was prepared to wink at his heresy rather than lose the presence of a young man so intellectually alert and so warm-hearted.[3]

Apart from his doctrinal dissent, however, James found himself totally out of sympathy with the atmosphere of the institution, with the manners and attitudes prevalent among the students. A smug professionalism possessed the place. The seminary struck him as producing Phariseeism instead of spirituality. One was led to view the world as divided into the righteous church-goers on the one hand, and on the other the sinners, for whom the Deity experienced only loathing and contempt. James felt that though a Christlike humility might be found among the technical sinners, it was indeed rare among the technical saints, in whom the pretension to righteousness in the eyes of God betokened the most flatulent self-satisfaction.

The seminarians began their career under the assumption that they were called to a holier sort of life than the laity. James' democratic soul detected the temper of the priest under the Protestant garb of his associates: they were at bottom, ritualists and ceremonialists. He winced at the histrionic element in their natures— 'that element of unconscious hypocrisy which Christ stigmatized in the religious zealots of his day, and which indeed seems to be inseparable from the religious *profession*. The ordinary theological student, especially, has a fatal professional conscience from the start, which vitiates his intellectual integrity. He is personally mortgaged to an *institution*—that of the pulpit—which is reputed sacred, and is all the more potent in its influence upon his natural freedom on that account; so that even the free sphere of his manners is almost sure to lose whatever frank spontaneous flavor it may by inheritance once have had, and become simply servile to convention.'⁴

In his *Nature of Evil*, James suspends an argument to characterize one of his professors whose beauty of character exhibited no stain but such as issued from his profession. 'Good old Dr Miller, of Princeton, used to say, in order to illustrate the force of his belief in the "federal headship" of Adam, that he had literally repented himself of that distant progenitor's sin. But the dear old man was of so sweet and courteous a disposition by nature, that his actual or proper sins gave him a sinecure almost, or had scarcely bulk enough to ruffle the placid current of his life; and he was consequently left all manner of leisure and inclination for acts of supererogatory and luxurious devotion. . . . A less mercenary, or more guileless piety than Dr Miller's I never knew, and he would have been universally reckoned a pattern of Christian manhood, if the extreme sweetness of his natural disposition, and the exquisite urbanity of his manners, by giving him so much superficial and secular sanctity as well, had not somewhat overlaid the depths of genuine humility in which his soul habitually dwelt.'[5]

James argued with his professors and his fellows. God's life in man, he thought, was surely not restricted to this petty theological world, with its allegations of heresy, its hinted suspicions of this one's orthodoxy, its concern about the technical whiteness of that one's own soul, its utter unconcern for the happiness and well-being of the whole human race as distinguished from the elect remnant. James writes of himself and his friend: 'we had both of us come to entertain some very fatal doubts as to the received theories in relation to the constitution of the Church, —our ecclesiastical guides holding, for example, that the Church was essentially a visible institution, defined and constituted mainly by the possession and ministry of the sacraments; while we maintained that it was an actual life of God himself in human nature, and not to be cogitated, therefore, apart from the interests of universal justice in the earth. . . .'[6]

James began to lose his sense of a distinction between the church and the world, to turn from the 'most literal and abject husks of Christian doctrine' to the 'truth of God's NATURAL HUMANITY, or identifying the honor of his name with the reverence of universal man.' Such an interpretation seemed to him the real meaning of Christianity; yet 'who,' he writes, 'is ever intellectually encouraged by the Church to universalize the Christian truth, and invest it with strictly humanitary dimensions?' [7] For himself, he began to find it difficult to say 'where his secular consciousness left off and his religious consciousness began.' His conversation unaffectedly spiritualized secular things and secularized spiritual. The ritual appurtenances of religion, even to grace at meals, grew burdensome to him; he 'had no technically religious conversation, never initiating nor indeed encouraging any discourse voluntarily attuned to the divine honor. . . .' [8]

He alarmed one and no doubt many a 'starched and complacent "brother"' at the seminary by his somewhat flippantly expressed unconcern about his future destiny. [9] What place could be found in the church for a young person who professed not the slightest curiosity over the alternative of salvation or damnation, heaven or hell; nor exhibited over his eschatological prospects the slightest concern?

II

During James' stay at the seminary, the Presbyterian denomination was suffering a vigorous theological controversy between conservatives and liberals, or Old

School and New. Eighteen hundred and thirty inaugurated seven years of strife. The 'Plan of Union' by
which in 1831 the Congregationalists and Presbyterians
had attained to a sort of federation had succeeded in
leavening conservative Presbyterianism with the liberal
New England theology emanating from New Haven.
The result was a series of trials for heresy instituted
against the Rev. Messrs Barnes, Duffield, and Beecher,
which evoked, upon both sides, the most intense feeling.[10]

Dr Samuel Miller, Princeton's Professor of Ecclesiastical History, forcefully enunciated the alarm and dis-
tress of the conservatives in a public letter. He re-
minded his readers that their denomination 'professes
to be a CALVINISTIC CHURCH,' and asserted that,
contrary to this profession, Pelagianism and Arminian-
ism were finding exponents and exposition. He charged
the New School with teaching: 'That we have no
more to do with the first sin of *Adam*, than with that
of any other parent:—that he was not constituted the
covenant head of his posterity, but was merely their
natural progenitor:—that there is no such thing as
original sin; that infants come into the world as perfectly free from corruption of nature, as *Adam* was
when he was created; . . . that by human depravity
is meant nothing more than the universal fact, that
all the posterity of *Adam*, though born entirely free
from universal defilement, will always begin to sin
when they begin to exercise moral agency; . . . that
the human will determines itself;—that the impeni-
tent sinner is by nature, in full possession of all the

powers necessary to a full compliance with all the commands of God; . . . that he elected men to eternal life, on a foresight of what their character would be. . . ." [11]

In order to preserve the pure faith of Calvinism un-sullied by these dreadful heresies, the Old School suc-ceeded, by 1838, in excising from the Church the liberal synods of New England and western New York. Princeton, with Professors Alexander and Miller, feel-ing general sympathy with the Old School, the liberals founded, at New York, the Union Seminary. [12]

The whole controversy must have inspired Henry James with a cordial distaste: the work of God in his world finding expression in humanitary impulse rather than in cerebral gestation. Yet in spite of his annoyance at theologians, James himself was an inveterate thinker and equally inveterate disputant; and controversy was a sweet savor to his nostrils.

One might have expected to find James ranged with the New School, but he must early have fallen into the fashion so redoubtably his in later life of con-stituting himself, on every topic under debate, a party of one. Having surveyed the rival forces, he proceeds to belabor both.

Orthodox theology 'supposes that God is literally enraged at man on account of his disobedience, and that He really inflicts suffering upon him from a just desire to give him pain, and that man consequently must be immeasurably unhappy to all eternity, unless this sanguinary demand of Deity become previously

appeased and surfeited in the blood of a superior vic-
tim. Of course the human mind cannot always rest
content under a programme of the Divine relations
so revolting as this.' The old doctrine of our Fall as
implicated in that of Adam, our 'federal head,' came
nevertheless to exercise a sedative effect: 'it was found
that the people in the pews, especially those who had
been long soaked in this doctrine, slept very soundly,
and were occasionally heard indeed to snore very
loudly, to its dulcet melody.' [13]

The New School, it is admitted, awakened the
slumbering, but to 'the unmitigated night of Pagan-
ism,' with 'every star of hope and consolation in the
tranquil Christian heavens blotted out.' They made
sin voluntary rather than essential; and they postulated
the autonomy of the human will. [14] In Jamesian terminology, they held sin to be *moral* rather than *spiritual*.

On the whole, James found more truth in orthodoxy,
with its insistence on the invincible grace of God, than
in liberalism, with its attribution of reality to human
selves. The Jamesian monism felt more affinity for
rigorous Calvinism than for the softer pluralisms that
were beginning to populate the theological world.

But whatever the choice of a system, it must be
one's own. And before choosing, one must have can-
vassed the possibilities. There may be varieties of
Christianity, even, not to be sampled at Princeton.

In search of greater liberty of thought and desirous
of henceforward seeking the life of God in man by
secular rather than priestly order, Henry James ob-

tained six months' leave of absence for a trip to England,[15] and left the seminary in 1837, never to return.

In a letter under the date of 1843, addressed to his friend, Joseph Henry, then Professor at Princeton,[16] James has put down his final impression of the seminary fold. I would, he writes, have run down to Princeton to see you, 'had it not been for the awkwardness of meeting people there who *will not talk with* one on equal terms, about those matters which necessarily form the only staple of discourse *with them*. I cannot so far stultify my understanding of the divine order as to suppose any human being or set of beings entitled by their attainments in philosophy or devotion to pass an *a priori* judgment upon those who chance to differ from them. The disgusting narrowness of church people afflicts my spirit with as palpable an asphyxia as charcoal vapour produces in my body; and effectually forbids all hope of pleasant or profitable intercourse with them. My recollection of the Princeton people is that they are virtuous, agreeable people up to a certain pitch: were it my lot to be thrown much with them I should suffer from a constant apprehension of that pitch becoming transcended, and of their turning out something quite otherwise.'

III

A correspondence between Henry James and Joseph Henry preserves the dates of James' first trip to England. He arrived at Plymouth on the 'Westminster' early in May, 1837, and sailed from Portsmouth on the 'Ontario' on September the twentieth of the same year. Professor Henry, who knew nothing of James' project of a visit to Europe, hoped his young friend would join him in Paris, and wrote another friend, Dr Bache,[17] requesting him to invite James to accompany him to Paris. James 'is a person to whom I am indebted for very special marks of friendship and would be pleased to serve while in Europe. I think it probable I will accompany him to the North. I mean to Edinburgh and Dublin. He has had the misfortune to lose one of his legs and on this account will be somewhat unpleasantly situated among strangers.'

The pleasures of the Continent were deferred. James replied to Henry:[18] 'I should very much like to go on to Paris with Bache, but fancy I shall be obliged to go into Ireland, and spend a few weeks with an uncle's family there. . . . The only things I care about seeing on the continent, seeing I should have such a short time to spend there, are Venice and Rome—but presume the malaria of those southern regions will keep me from visiting either during the summer.'

Henry's fear for James' discomfort failed to reckon with his friend's invincible blitheness. 'I have commenced my arrangements for getting a good cork leg', the young man mentions; and he concludes, 'I feel a little homesick occasionally—but in the main do charmingly—spend my time pretty much in my room, and am as happy generally as the day is long.'

The journey to Ireland, concerning the necessity of which James wrote his friend, was effected; and *Notes of a Son and Brother* incorporates a brief and glamorous if somewhat fanciful account of the 'few weeks with an uncle's family,' at Bailieborough, County Cavan, the birthplace of the elder William James.[19] Though their tombstones show the family to have been one of the first families of the village, their status did not exceed that of tenant farmers; and Henry, as the son and representative of the incredibly successful and wealthy emigrant, must have created a local stir; but the principal sensation appears to have been produced by the 'almost epic shape' of Billy Taylor, the black man-servant who had accompanied Henry from Albany.

IV

What Henry James saw and experienced during this sojourn in England we do not know: record remains but of its intellectual consequence,—the espousal of the Sandemanian gospel. Mr Robert Sandeman, 'that respectable Scottish sectary,'[20] had died at the Connecticut village of Danbury more than sixty years before, but his sect continued in existence; and among them Mr James found an adumbration of the views which were beginning to take shape in his own mind.

It seems altogether likely that James first encountered Sandemanianism in the person of its most eminent (perhaps one could say its single eminent) adherent, Michael Faraday. At Faraday's death in 1867, William

White, brilliant English Swedenborgian, writes to James:[21] 'You had some curious intercourse with him which I wish you would place on record. If you are too busy to do so, I wish you would commit your memories to your son who writes for the press. Faraday, I dare say, was of no account as a mental philosopher, but as a man of science his merits were altogether unique. . . .'

The request evoked from James a reply which is lost; to it White in turn replies, 'What you write about Faraday quite confirms the conception I had formed of his intellectual religious condition.' The comment makes it clear that the intercourse between James and Faraday concerned itself, as from James' obsession we should expect, with theology. James was early concerned with the relations of science and religion; and it seems perfectly natural that he should have sought out the distinguished scientist who was at the same time the most simple and devout of Christians. An introduction could readily have been his through Joseph Henry, whose professional interests paralleled Faraday's and who spent much time with him in London.[22]

In their practises, as well as in their doctrine, the Sandemanians professed a return to primitive Christianity. Some of these specialities, the weekly celebration of the Lord's supper, the love feast, the kiss of charity, abstinence from blood and things strangled, the washing of the brethren's feet, could scarcely have aroused much interest in James; but with the spirit which prompted them—the desire to return to the simple ways of the earlier church, to put brotherly love and the fellowship of believers before doctrinal quibbles and dogmatic professions, he would have had much sympathy. The Sandemanians' Christian Socialism, their belief in community of goods, 'so far as that every one is to consider all he has in his possession and power liable to the calls of the poor and the church',[23] would have made a strong appeal to James. And, most important perhaps, the Sandemanians, like the Quakers, tolerated no paid and professional clergy; laymen, elected by lot (Faraday was once of their number), served as elders. Such an arrangement could not but win the approval of the vehement young enemy of 'priests' and organized churches.

In his days at Princeton, James had disputed with his professors concerning the fundamental doctrine of 'justification by faith.' Among the Sandemanians he found a different and more straightforward conception of the nature of faith. *Faith* is equivalent to *belief*, they taught: as used by the apostles it bears the same meaning as in common discourse—a persuasion of the truth of a proposition; so that 'there is no difference between believing any common testimony and believing the apostolic testimony, except that which results from the testimony itself, and the divine authority on which it rests.'[24]

But more than anything else, James was attracted by Sandeman's conception of the relation between morality and religion, as developed, with a vigor and

brilliance of style which suggest, to a degree, James'
own, in Letters on Theron and Aspasio.[25] Like James,
Sandeman felt only contempt for those who found
morality ultimate, or who supposed that in the eyes
of the Deity there was respect of persons. The Pharisee,
or moralist, fancies himself acceptable to God because
of his own righteousness; the publican, or true Christian, knows that only his humility and his utter un-
worthiness can win him mercy.

All the great revivers of apostolic zeal—St Augustine,
Luther, Calvin—have preached that works without
faith are vain; that sheer grace, and not antecedent
respectability, is the instrument of salvation; that Christ
has come to call 'sinners, not the righteous.'[26] But
though these articles of belief continue to stand in the
official theologies, the decline of Christian fervor and
the increase of worldliness among Christians bring
inevitably a popular Pelagianism which spreads from
pulpit to pew—the belief that religion is just a new
edition of morality; that Christianity, instead of being folly to the strong and aberration to the wise, but
republishes the maxims of Moses and Confucius.

Sandeman, like James, feels that, in popular preach-
ing and popular religion, character rather than sheer
grace, righteousness rather than redemption, is made
the means of salvation; and, like James, he inveighs
against 'moralism.'

Of grace and works, Sandeman writes: 'Paul, when
speaking of the sovereignty of the Divine choice of
men to salvation, as proceeding upon grace, in opposi-

tion to every notion of desert in those who are chosen, distinguishes that grace in the following manner: *And if by grace, then it is no more of works; otherwise grace is no more grace; but if it be of works, then is it no more grace.* . . . If this one text were well understood, the whole body of the popular doctrine would fall to the ground at once.' 'No doctrine in Scripture wears a more amiable and inviting aspect to the self-condemned, than that of the Divine sovereignty, as described by Paul, in his Epistle to the Romans. . . . This removes every cause of despair to the most wretched of mankind. For who can be led to despair by the view of any deficiency about himself whatever, who knows that none but the utterly deficient are chosen by God to salvation? As no doctrine is more encouraging than this to the miserable, so none is more provoking to the sons of pride, who want to stand upon their distinctions before God, and are not yet reduced so low as to be entirely at mercy for their Salvation.' 'The popular preachers are greatly disgusted at this doctrine. . . . Here no man's pride is flattered; no man can find any ground to presume that the Deity regards him more than others.'

The 'characters' of the Pharisees and Jesus aroused much ire among the 'popular preachers.' Sandeman asserts that the Pharisees were not 'worse men than ourselves.' Even the Lord granted 'that they outwardly *appeared righteous* unto men, and speaks of them as *highly esteemed* among men, who knew as well how to judge of characters as we do. . . . The chief thing for which we find them censured in the New Testament, is, that they presumed God had a peculiar regard for them, and would accept them on account of the excellency of their lives': they 'presumed, that what distinguished them from other men, would recommend them to God.' Jesus 'regarded not the difference from other men which the Pharisees made so much account of: though Christians early became 'ashamed of this part of Christ's character.' He made friends rather of sinners than of the righteous.[27]

Of this rather violent antinomianism a New England divine declared with some truth: Sandeman tries to 'persuade us, with the most artful touches, that every *appearance of devotion and righteousness, is the mark of the Pharisee; that Jesus Christ shewed the highest indignation against all virtue, and especially against those good works which are highly esteemed among men; and that the conversion of a sinner is always effected in such a supernatural way, as entirely excludes all previous means, endeavours, or preparations of the heart, either by our own labor, or any operations of the Holy Spirit upon the understanding or conscience.'[28] But Sandeman's invective against 'moralism' appears again, and with heightened powers of raillery and vituperation, in the books of Mr James.

There is, then, point in the circumstance that James' first publication was an edition of Sandeman's *Letters,* brought out in 1838, immediately after his return to America. The brief, unsigned preface, dated at New York,[29] appears to be addressed, in part at least, to the Presbyterians whose fold the editor had so recently abandoned. Characteristic touches are the defiant mention of 'the severity of censure which SANDEMAN saw fit to indulge towards the most venerated names of his day' and the proclamation, in similar temper, that Sandeman's name 'has long been under reproach, and will probably so continue while the memory of these letters shall endure.'

James soon abandoned Sandeman for other masters; and in his books he never mentions the name. But Sandeman's contribution to the thought of his young American disciple was nevertheless a significant one.

CHAPTER III

EMERSON

I

In 1840, James entered into a marriage which was to furnish the surest of foundations for an extraordinarily rich family life and which gave the head of the family that love and confidence which his deeply affectionate nature craved. Mary James was the sister of Hugh Walsh, who entered the Princeton Theological Seminary in 1835 along with Henry James, and, sharing his friend's doubts, left it after somewhat more than a year, to become a physician.[1] Lacking the dialectic or wit of her husband and sons, without that combination of the philosophical and the literary which marks them all, she lived in her family and for them without in the slightest sinking into a mere docile domesticity. 'We simply lived by her,' writes her son Henry, 'in proportion as we lived spontaneously, with an equanimity of confidence, an independence . . . which left us free for detachments of thought and flights of mind, experiments so to speak, on the assumption of our genius and our intrinsic interest. . . . This was a support on which my father rested with the absolute whole of his weight. . . . She lived in ourselves so exclusively, with such a want of use for anything in her consciousness that was not about us and for us, that I think we almost contested her being separate enough to be proud of us—it was too like our being proud of ourselves.'²

James bought a house at number 21 Washington Place, New York. Here his two eldest children, William and Henry, were born in 1842 and 1843.

He continued his theological studies, undertaking in particular to read the Bible for himself and make of it what he could. His exploration of *Genesis* suggested to his mind that its early chapters were mystical rather than scientific, intended not to 'throw a direct light upon our natural or race history' but to reveal in symbolic form 'the laws of God's *spiritual* creation and providence.'³ Indeed, his own reflexions at this period adumbrated the doctrine of correspondence he was soon to find systematically put in Swedenborg; for in 1843 he writes his friend, Professor Henry: 'Again and again I am forced by scriptural philosophy to the conviction that all the phenomena of physics are to be explained and grouped under laws *exclusively spiritual*—that they are in fact only the material expression of spiritual truth—or as Paul says the visible forms of invisible substance. Heb. 11.3.'⁴ He wrote a course of lectures in exposition

of these ideas and delivered them to good audiences in
New York, and the search for the secret of the universe went on. James inquired diligently of all who
professed to have discovered it; and the years in the
neighborhood of 1840 were years fertile in new Mes-
siahs and new gospels.

II

Once he seemed to have found his prophet. A
spare New Englander came to New York to lecture; [5] and the tone and spirit of the man, still more
than what he said, bespoke a *spiritual* authority beyond the reach of scribes.

Of all the men who felt the charm and power of
Emerson, not even Lowell has left on record a more
vivid description of his performance as lecturer. 'His
demeanour upon the platform . . . was modesty itself: not the mere absence of display, but the presence
of a positive personal grace. His deferential entrance
upon the scene, his look of inquiry at the desk and
the chair, his resolute rummaging among his em-
barrassed papers, the air of sudden recollection with
which he would plunge into his pockets for what
he must have known had never been put there, his
uncertainty and irresolution as he rose to speak, his
deep, relieved inspiration as he got well from under
the burning-glass of his auditors' eyes, and addressed
himself at length to their docile ears instead: no
maiden ever appealed more potently to your enamoured and admiring sympathy. And then when he

looked over the heads of his audience into the dim mysterious distance, and his weird monotone began to reverberate in your bosom's depths, and his words flowed on, now with a river's volume, grand, majestic, free, and anon diminished themselves to the fitful cadence of a brook, impeded in its course, and returning in melodious coquetry upon itself, and you saw the clear eye eloquent with nature's purity, and beheld the musing countenance turned within, as it were, and hearkening to the rumour of a far-off but oncoming world: how intensely personal, how exquisitely characteristic, it all was!'[6]

To this unknown friend of those who would live in the spirit, James resolved to put his case. He wrote Emerson:

'MY DEAR SIR,

I listened to your address this evening, and as my bosom glowed with many a true word that fell from your lips I felt ere long fully assured that before me I beheld a man who in very truth was seeking the realities of things. . . . I will write to him that I too in my small degree am coveting to understand the truth which surrounds me and embraces me, am seeking worthily to apprehend—or to be more worthily apprehended of—the love which underlies and vivifies all the seeming barrenness of our most unloving world; but that yet for every step I have taken I find myself severed from friends and kindred. . . . I will further tell him that to talk familiarly with one who earnestly follows truth through whatever frowning ways she beckons him on . . . has never been my lot for one half hour even; and that he

therefore, if he be now the generous lover of truth and
of her friends which he seems to be, may give me this
untasted pleasure, and let me once feel the cordial grasp
of a fellow-pilgrim. . . .'⁷

The appeal found its response. Emerson called
upon the Jameses, was taken upstairs (so the tradition runs) to bestow his blessing upon the infant
William.⁸ Thereafter Emerson and James corresponded; and when New York furnished his platform, the lecturer from Concord abode with the
James family.

Emerson found James and his household refuge
indeed. He writes in his Journals, 'I have made no
note of these long weary absences at New York and
Philadelphia. I am a bad traveller, and the hotels
are mortifications to all sense of well-being in me.
The people who fill them oppress me with their excessive virility, and would soon become intolerable
if it were not for a few friends, who, like women,
tempered the acrid mass. Henry James was true comfort,—wise, gentle, polished, with heroic manners,
and a serenity like the sun.'⁹

Son Henry could recall one of these visits: 'the
winter firelight of our back-parlour at dusk and the
great Emerson—I knew he was greater, greater than
any of our friends—sitting in it between my parents . . . as an apparition sinuously and, I held,
elegantly slim, benevolently aquiline, and command-
ing a tone alien, beautifully alien, to any we heard
roundabout. . . .'¹⁰

III

Swedenborg tells us of angels celestial and angels spiritual,—beings, the highest, who live from love, and beings, secondary, who live from truth. Though it was the celestial life, the innocent, spontaneous life of the affections, for which James was all his days impassionedly to plead, he was himself of the spiritual genius, enamoured of dialectic, possessed by a never-flagging impulse to articulate metaphysically the truths about the celestial character of love.

Emerson alternately inspired and disappointed his metaphysical friend. Clearly the 'new man' of the super-moral order which was at any moment to be ushered in, he totally lacked the power to interpret himself and could give no array of reasons for believing as he did. Intuition, not argument, was his organ of apprehension.

Intellectually, then, James found him quite unsatisfactory. And this feeling emerges clearly from a pair of letters James wrote. He tells his friend candidly: 'All that I can at present say is that being better satisfied with you than any man I ever met, I am worst satisfied: which being interpreted means, that while your *life* is of that sort which, so far as I can detect it, lays hold of my profoundest love, ever and anon some provokingly perverse way of speech breaks forth which does not seem to me to come from the life, and incontinently knocks me into downright *pi* again.' [11] 'Oh, you man without a *handle!*'

he ejaculates at another time. 'Shall one never be able to help himself out of you, according to his needs, and be dependent only upon your fitful tip-pings-up?' [12]

James articulates the gravamen of his complaint against the seer most clearly in an epistle addressed 'To the Invisible Emerson.' 'I,' he writes, 'am led . . . to seek the *laws* of these appearances that swim round us in God's great museum, to get hold of some central facts which may make all other facts properly circumferential and orderly; and you con-tinually dishearten me by your apparent indifference to such law and such facts, by the dishonor you seem to cast on our intelligence, as if it were what stands in our way. Now, my conviction is that my intelli-gence is the necessary digestive apparatus for my life; that there is nihil in vita—worth anything, that is—quod non prius in intellectu. Now is it not so in truth with you? Can you not report your life to me by some intellectual symbol which my intel-lect appreciates?' [13]

The letter ends with a confession of the writer's own sad plight. 'Here I am these thirty-one years in life, ignorant in all outward science, but having patient habits of meditation which never know dis-gust or weariness, and feeling a force of impulsive love toward all humanity which will not let me rest wholly mute. . . . What shall I do? Shall I get me a little nook in the country and communicate with my *living* kind—not my talking kind—by life only;

a word perhaps of *that* communication, a fit word
once a year? Or shall I follow some commoner
method—learn science and bring myself first into
man's respect, that I may thus the better speak to
him?'

Emerson's replies make no attempt at replying
either to the passion or to the intellect of the appeals:
their tone is personal. The admired 'will not conceal'
his pleasure at James' abiding interest in him. Intimation that the whole family may betake themselves
to Europe arouses some glow of sentiment:

'I hear of your plans of travelling with a kind
of selfish alarm, as we do of the engagement of beautiful women who shall now shine no more on us.
We talked along so comfortably together, and the
madness (is it?) you find in my logic made such
good antagonism, that New York looked greatly
nearer and warmer to me for your inhabitation.'[14]

IV

Emerson was eager to introduce his new friend to
such others as he most esteemed and loved.

After living two years in Emerson's household,
Thoreau was going to the city to try his fortune.
Emerson recommends him to James' attention. He
is 'a profound mind and a person of true magnanim-
ity, and if it should happen that there is some village
pedantry and tediousness of facts, it will easily be
forgotten when you come at what is better. . . .'[15]

Two months later Emerson reports to James being
'greatly gratified' by 'Henry Thoreau's joy in your
company. He said he stood a catechism that was as
good as a bath and seemed to find a compensation
for the whole disappointment of the city, which he
does not love.'[16]

There is Thoreau's own account of this same
catechetical 'bath' in a letter to Emerson, June 8,
1843: 'I have been to see Henry James, and I like
him very much. It was a great pleasure to meet
him. It makes humanity seem more erect and respectable. I never was more kindly and faithfully
catechized. It made me respect myself more to be
thought worthy of such wise questions. He is a man,
and takes his own way, or stands still in his own
place. I know of no one so patient and determined
to have the good of you. It is almost friendship, such
plain and human dealing. . . . He actually reproaches
you by his respect for your poor words. I had three
hours' solid talk with him, and he asks me to make
free use of his house.'[17]

Thoreau was to be bearer of Emerson's only demand upon James' mind. 'I want that he should tell
you about our Dial, which has just escaped the fate
of being extinguished. Can you not send me some
brief record of your faith or hope to enliven our
little journal with a new element?'[18]

Another emissary from New England to New York
was Margaret Fuller, who joined the staff of Mr
Greeley's *Tribune* in 1844. Just before he is to sail for

Europe, James writes of her to Emerson, surely the
instrument of their meeting: 'I assure you it seems
a real hardship to go away out of the country now
that I have just come to talk with her. The dear noble
woman! I shall often think of her with joy—and
with hope of fuller conferences and sympathies somewhere.' [19]

Theodore Parker, the theological *enfant terrible* of
Boston, was a welcome guest always.

When Bronson Alcott came to New York to hold
his 'conversations,' he habitually visited Mr James.
There was much about Alcott both to offend and
to amuse his host. A journalist has reported one of
their conversations accurately enough. Calling upon
James one day, Alcott said: 'Life is the dispersion
of the identities, and the concentration of the diversi-
ties.' Mr James gave a different statement, and the
two were 'deep in mysticism' [the reporter's description!] in no time. Mr Alcott could not condone the
attempt to translate his sayings into common sense,
and said abruptly to Mr James, 'You'll continue a
sinner to all eternity; you are damaged goods.' He
claimed that he himself was one with Pythagoras
and Jesus. The three had never sinned, and had all
that advantage over other men. Mr James pushed
his point: 'You say you and Jesus are one. Have you
ever said "I am the resurrection and the life"?' 'Yes,
often,' was the reply. 'Has any one ever believed you?'
The conversation here ended abruptly, Mr Alcott
saying, 'I won't talk any more with you.' [20]

Whatever their 'mystical' differences, James' personal relations with Alcott were ever 'most frank, cordial and friendly';[21] and the fact that Carlyle early adopted Alcott as a butt for satire aroused James' sense of justice to persistent protest that, if Alcott had been 'innocent enough, and indiscreet enough, to affront conventional prejudice by assuming a mystical sort of equality with the most renowned name on the bead-roll of men's reverential memory,' Carlyle was surely not given to placating either orthodox or Philistines.

V

It was doubtless Emerson who brought Carlyle's writing to his attention. In 1843 James writes Emerson: 'I am cheered by the coming of Carlyle's new book [*Past and Present*]. . . . The title is provokingly enigmatical, but thought enough there will be in it no doubt, whatever the name; thought heaped up to topheaviness and inevitable lopsidedness, but more interesting to me than comes from any other quarter of Europe—interesting for the man's sake whom it shows. According to my notion he is the very best interpreter of a spiritual philosophy that could be devised for *this age*. . . . Just to think of a Scotchman with a heart widened to German spiritualities! . . . You don't look upon Calvinism as a fact at all; wherein you are to my mind philosophically infirm—impaired in your universality. I can see in Carlyle the advantage his familiarity with it gives him over you with a general audience. What is highest in him is built upon that lowest. At least so I read; I believe Jonathan Edwards redivivus in true blue would, after an honest study of the philosophy that has grown up since his day, make the best possible reconciler and critic of this philosophy— far better than Schelling redivivus.' [22]

When James left for England, in October, 1843, Emerson provided him with introductions to his English friends, notably John Sterling and Carlyle. He writes to Sterling that James is 'at once so manly, so intelligent, and so ardent that I have found him . . . a chief consolation to me when I visit his city,' [23] and to Carlyle, 'Lately went Henry James to you with a letter from me. He is a fine companion from his intelligence, valor, and worth, and is and has been a very beneficent person as I learn.' [24]

Carlyle's favorable impression of James is recorded in letters written not long after. In November he assures Emerson, 'James is a very good fellow, better and better as we see him more. Something shy and skittish in the man; but a brave heart intrinsically, with sound, earnest sense, with plenty of insight and even humor. He confirms an observation of mine . . . that a stammering man is never a worthless one. . . . James is now off to the Isle of Wight; will see Sterling at Ventnor there. . . .' [25] And he asks Sterling in December: 'Did you see an American of the name of James, who went towards you? An estimable man, full of sense and honest manfulness, when you get acquainted with him.' [26]

The Carlyles' house, into which James now had entry, was the habitual resort of the chief free-thinkers of England. There the American met Wilkinson, Mill, Maurice, Tennyson, Spedding, Arthur Helps, Lewes, Baldwin Brown, Sterling. And he met them, as he met everyone, with abundant friendliness for the man, but the most vigilant criticism of his doctrine. [27]

At the end of his life James recalled this company. 'Maurice disappointed me very much. I wanted to talk with him, but he wouldn't talk. He perhaps felt that my views were pestilent. He seemed narrow outside the pale of the church.

'Mr Mill was the best of the lot, except Sterling, who was the truest man I ever met. There was a great deal of the woman in him—a lovely person. . . . Sterling was a perfectly delightful man, just the antipodes of Carlyle and the only man Carlyle had any sincere attachment to. Sterling was the only man in England who seemed like an American in spirit and manners. He was then near the end of his life [Sterling died in 1844]. He talked freely, was jocund, very full of life, and was dying in perfect confidence, with no knowledge of the future and no beliefs.

'Mr Mill was the most sincere man I ever met.' In *Substance and Shadow,* James pauses between his berating of Kant and Sir William Hamilton and his gentler rebuke to Mill the metaphysician, to praise the character of Mill, 'a man in my judgment of far superior intellectual breadth to any of the persons I have been discussing. His intellect appears to me thoroughly penetrated and vivified by his heart; and though his opinions may reflect to some extent the defects of his early doctrinal training, one easily feels how small a matter that is beside the profound humanity which underlies all his judgments. In all Mr Mill's books one feels the man very much more than the author; feels the upright human heart throbbing to such purpose, that he is certain the somewhat narrow systematic head will one day or other encounter the necessary enlargement. How can any one read that noble book of his upon Liberty without conceiving the liveliest respect and affection for the writer; it is so sincere, generous, and full of manly sympathy for the wants of the time.' [28]

As for the rest: 'Mr Spedding was sincere, modest and bore his part ably in discussions with Carlyle. Mr Helps was in delicate health, but always charming. . . . These men, however, take them all in all, differed widely from Americans of the same type of thought. They had not half the seriousness of our men. Life to them began and ended in conversation, not in action. They never thought that Christ's spiritual life among men was of any consequence. They were cynical—all cynical but Sterling and Mill. . . . Their talk was depraving to the last degree. What they had to say was not a tenth part so inter-

esting as the talk you can have in America with the
person sitting next you in the horse cars.'

Carlyle, for all his simplicity and sincerity of manner, his hospitality, his gruff friendliness, proved almost total disappointment. Hailed by his admirers
as a man of ideas, he struck James as hardly advanced
beyond the stage of instinct. Acclaimed as a humani-
tarian, he lacked all positive hope in God or practical
love to man. He abounded in pity for his friends:
'"Poor John Sterling," he used always to say; "poor
John Mill, poor Frederic Maurice, poor Neuberg, poor
Arthur Helps, poor little Browning, poor little Lewes,"
and so on; as if the temple of his friendship were a
hospital, and all its inmates scrofulous or paralytic.'
But he never transcended pity and sympathy for
the individual. 'He scoffed with hearty scorn at the
contented imbecility of Church and State with respect to social problems, but his own indifference to
these things, save in so far as they were available to
picturesque palaver, was infinitely more indolent and
contented.' [29] Men who took an active interest in the
progress of humanity at large struck him as fanatics.
'A moral reformer like Louis Blanc or Robert Dale
Owen, a political reformer like Mr Cobden or Mr
Bright, or a dietetic reformer like the late Mr Greaves
or our own Mr Alcott, was sure to provoke his most
acrid intellectual antipathy.' [30]

Carlyle indeed was himself 'wont to question established institutions and dogmas with the utmost
license of scepticism, but he obviously meant nothing

beyond the production of a certain literary surprise, or the enjoyment of his own aesthetic power. Nothing maddened him so much as to be mistaken for a reformer, really intent upon the interests of God's righteousness upon the earth, which are the interests of universal justice. This is what made him hate Americans, and call us a nation of bores,—that we took him at his word, and reckoned upon him as a sincere well-wisher to his species.' [31]

No one, even Carlyle, ever called Henry James a bore. James' hearty good humor, his ready wit, his range of interests precluded that; and his hopes for the world avowed no sectarian tenets, depended for their fulfillment upon no single practical reform. But in his journals James recalled some real 'Disciples of the Newness' such as abounded in the America of the 1840's and, come to England, made their way to Chelsea. No one had a keener eye for absurdity than James; and his sadly preposterous fellow-pilgrims must, under the circumstances, have called for laughter. Carlyle's attitude, provocative of such obvious resentment from James, put that out of the question. These pathetic and ridiculous American reformers, whatever they lacked in humanistic balance, in urbanity of deportment, had attached themselves with invincible seriousness to the cause of humanity; and Carlyle, for all his genius, was not worthy to unlace their shoe-latchets.

CHAPTER IV

SWEDENBORG

I

THE sojourn in England involved no break in all-absorbing intellectual preoccupations; the Biblical and theological studies were pursued with unabated zeal. No doubt the zeal was too intense and too constant, for in the spring of 1844 Mr James experienced what may be regarded, according to one's psychology, as either a nervous breakdown or a conversion: it may be that one is not obliged to choose between the two. An extreme personal debility, an utter emptying of one's own resources, a 'vastation' of strength and pride: all this is preparatory to the ingress of the spirit. Purgation precedes illumination.

In Mr James' case, the two parts of the 'conversion' were separated by a very considerable interval of time, the vastation of self long anticipating the final influx of the Divine. The Law convicted him of sin long before the Gospel pronounced its gracious assurance of redemption.

Thus he describes the *vastation*: 'towards the close of May, having eaten a comfortable dinner, I remained sitting at the table after the family had dispersed, idly gazing at the embers in the grate, thinking of nothing, and feeling only the exhilaration incident to a good digestion, when suddenly—in a lightning-flash as it were—"fear came upon me, and trembling, which made all my bones to shake." To all appearances it was a perfectly insane and abject terror, without ostensible cause, and only to be accounted for, to my perplexed imagination, by some damned shape squatting invisible to me within the precincts of the room, and raying out from his fetid personality influences fatal to life. The thing had not lasted ten seconds before I felt myself a wreck, that is, reduced from a state of firm, vigorous, joyful manhood to one of almost helpless infancy. The only self-control I was capable of exerting was to keep my seat. I felt the greatest desire to run incontinently to the foot of the stairs and shout for help to my wife, —to run to the roadside even, and appeal to the public to protect me; but by an immense effort I controlled these frenzied impulses, and determined not to budge from my chair till I had recovered my lost self-possession. This purpose I held to for a good long hour, as I reckoned time, beat upon meanwhile by an ever-growing tempest of doubt, anxiety, and despair, with absolutely no relief from any truth I had ever encountered save a most pale and distant glimmer of the Divine existence,—when I resolved to abandon the vain struggle, and communicate without more ado what seemed my sudden burden of inmost, implacable unrest to my wife.'[1]

Consulting physicians, James was advised that he had overworked his brain, and that he should resort, for recovery, to the water-cure treatment. He betook himself to a celebrated 'cure,' which of itself, as he wittily says, 'did nothing towards curing my malady but enrich my memory with a few morbid specimens of English insularity and prejudice.' From the 'dismal water-cure' and 'endless "strife of tongues" about diet, and regimen, and disease, and politics, and parties, and persons' in which the invalidic frequenters of the springs indulged, James turned away in distaste and disgust. Momentarily, he longed to 'turn and live with the animals': *The curse of mankind, that which keeps our manhood so little and so depraved, is its sense of selfhood, and the absurd, abominable opinionativeness it engenders. How sweet it would be to find oneself no longer man, but one of those innocent and ignorant sheep pasturing upon that placid hillside, and drinking in eternal dew and freshness from Nature's lavish bosom!*[2]

His confidence in his selfhood, in his own powers, mental and moral, was completely broken. He preserved not the slightest faith in the 'immense piles of manuscript' which he had accumulated in the pursuance of his theological studies. It was borne in upon him, with increasing conviction, that man cannot by searching find out God—in His character either of

Love or of Truth. 'I suppose if any one had designated me previous to that event [the vastation] as an earnest seeker after truth, I should myself have seen nothing unbecoming in the appellation. But now, within two or three months of my catastrophe, I felt sure I had never caught a glimpse of truth. . . . Indeed, an ugly suspicion had more than once forced itself upon me that I had never really wished the truth, but only to ventilate my own ability in discovering it. . . . My studious mental activity had served manifestly to base a mere "castle in the air," and the castle had vanished in a brief moment of time, leaving not a wrack behind. I never felt again the most passing impulse, even, to look where it stood, having done with it forever. Truth, indeed! How should a beggar like me be expected to discover it? How should any man of woman born pretend to such ability? Truth must *reveal itself* if it would be known; and even then how imperfectly known at best!' Mr James' obscurantism echoes the Pauline: the world by wisdom knew not God.

Relief came through the medium of a certain gracious and charming Mrs Chichester, who lived in the vicinity of the water-cure—a lady 'of rare qualities of heart and mind, and of singular personal loveliness as well.'[3] To Mr James' story of his malady she brought an understanding hitherto unfurnished: and her friend was, she pronounced, undergoing what Swedenborg had called a *vastation*. Pressed for further enlightenment, she preluded her summary ex-

position of the Swedenborgian philosophy with modest confession of amateurism, but earnestly recom-
mended the reading of her author.

James hastened to London, visited his bookseller,
and from the array of tomes proffered him selected
the two slightest, *Divine Love and Wisdom* and
Divine Providence.[4]

It was at this time that he made the personal acquaintance of Dr Garth Wilkinson, Swedenborgian
of independent mind and robust personality. James'
attention had first been called to Wilkinson in 1841,
when the latter published, in Heraud's magazine,
Coleridge's marginalia upon Swedenborg, adding to
them a criticism of his own.[5] The men became intimate friends and regular correspondents.[6] James
named his third son, born in 1845, after his new
friend. Wilkinson dedicated to James his *Human
Body and its Connexion with Man* (1851); James'
Christianity the Logic of Creation (1851) consists of
'spiritual letters' addressed to Wilkinson, and the book
is inscribed to him.

From this time forward, Swedenborg was James'
constant companion. Henry recalls his father's 'vast,
even though incomplete, array of Swedenborg's works,
the old faded covers of which, anciently red, actually apt to be loose, and backed with labels of impressive, though to my sense somewhat sinister London imprint, Arcana Coelestia, Heaven and Hell and
other such matters. . . .' The volumes moved about
with the family on its peregrinations: they 'ranged

themselves before us wherever, and however briefly, we disposed ourselves, forming, even for short journeys, the base of our father's travelling library. . . . I recall them as inveterately part of our very luggage, requiring proportionate receptacles.' Upon the return from a journey, 'The Swedenborgs were promptly out again on their customary shelves or sometimes more improvised perches, and it was somehow not till we had assured ourselves of this that we felt that incident closed.'⁷

II

James' relation to Swedenborg was to be as exceptional as intense. Never ceasing to admire and to interpret, he denied assent either to the customary laudation of the man or to any of the existing expositions of his thought; and he steadfastly refused to ally himself with any of the several ecclesiasticisms which others had created to promote the study of the philosopher.

James celebrates the grandeur of Swedenborg: 'his vast erudition, untouched by pedantry, and never for an instant lending itself to display; his guileless modesty under the most unexampled experiences; his tender humility and ready fellowship with every lowest form of good; the free, unconscious movement of his thought, reflected from the great calm realities with which he was in habitual intellectual contact; his unstudied speech bubbling up at times into a childish *naïveté* and simplicity,—all these things,

while they take his books out of the category of mere
literary performance, and convert them into an epoch,
as it were, of our associated mental history, . . . yet
assuredly reduce the feats of our sincerest theologians
and philosophers to the dimensions of ignorant prat-
tle, and turn the performances of our ordinary literary posturemongers into stale and mercenary circus
tricks.' [8]

But to attribute to Swedenborg some personal ab-
solutism, some doctrinal infallibility, James refused.
'Swedenborg's natural cast of mind is utterly unau-
thoritative, utterly averse, not merely to command,
but even to persuade; so that if any one will insist
upon having an infallible guide as to the truths his
own great mind *ought* to acknowledge, and the goods
his own large heart *ought* to cherish, Swedenborg is not
the least in the world the man he is in search of.'
James ascribes no more dogmatic authority to him
'than I should ascribe in their various measure to
Socrates and John Mill.' Acceptance of Swedenborg's
principles and pronouncements depends upon the appeal to religious experience, not to authority. 'The
sphere of Revelation is the sphere of life exclusively,
and its truth is addressed not to the reflective understanding of men but to their living perception. Truth,
to every soul that has ever felt its inward breathing, disowns all outward authority. . . .' [9]

James evinced no blindness to the limitations of his
seer. Much of Emerson's brilliant essay on Swedenborg amounts to saying that his subject was scientist

and theologian, not man of letters, not rhetorician.
To the qualification, James cheerfully assents. On
the surface the *theological works* 'repel delight. They
would seem to have been mercifully constructed on
the plan of barring out idle acquaintance, and disgusting a voluptuous literary curiosity.' The books
are 'singularly void of literary fascination. I know
of no writer with anything like his [Swedenborg's]
intellectual force who is so persistently feeble in point
of argumentative or persuasive skill. His books teem
with the grandest, the most humane and generous
truth; but his reverence for it is so austere and vital,
that, like the lover who willingly makes himself of
no account beside his mistress, he seems always intent
upon effacing himself from sight before its matchless
lustre.' [10]

James did not busy himself with controversy over
Swedenborg's claim or the claims of his followers
for him. Whether the Seer was technically sane or
insane appeared a matter of indifference to one who
judged metaphysical truth a province distinct from
biography. And the veracity of a man who professed to write of Heaven and Hell from personal
observation was to be doubted only if what he reported lacked consonance with one's own deepest
reading of the present life.

Sure that, though there were many and various
interpretations of Swedenborg, he himself had found
the correct one, James did not seriously deny that he
was an interpreter, that he selected from the abun-

dance of materials, that he developed. More, he denied that intelligent persons could do otherwise; he felt only contempt for the parroting of line and verse which passed as homage to the Seer.[11]

Swedenborg, says James, is not a thinker; he is 'at best a mere informer or reporter, though an egregiously intelligent one, in the interest of a new evolution of the human mind, speculative and practical . . .'; he had no prophetic faculty. 'He is in no way remarkable as a man of original thought, or even as a reasoner, unless it be negatively so. . . . His judgments doubtless in regard to this world's affairs were those of his day and generation, and strike one as grown very antiquated. . . .'[12]

A metaphor puts the case positively. 'His books, in fact, amount to nothing so much as to an intellectual wheatfield, of no use to any one who does not enter in to gather and bind his own golden sheaves, and then proceed to thresh and grind his grain, to bolt his flour, to mix his bread, to build it up and bake it in such shapely and succulent loaves as his own intellectual bread-pan alone determines.'[13]

The voluminousness of Swedenborg's writings, their very apparent difficulty, and the very various readings men of parts have given them, have made students of James timid about proclaiming his exegesis of Swedenborg the 'real right' one. An intelligent reviewer of his thinks: 'Whether Mr James' doctrine is purely Swedenborg's, or in fact his own liberal interpretation of Swedenborg, is more than we can venture

to conclude. Certainly, we find Swedenborg very
plainly asserting doctrines which seem to us very
narrow, and by no means according with the generous
and broad estimate Mr James makes of his theology.
. . . These and other passages that might be cited
from Swedenborg's writings Mr James would surely
find it difficult to explain away or to reconcile with
the doctrine which he himself continually presents,
that Christianity is a life, and not a dogma; and with
the extremely liberal views of evil and of hell
given. . . .' [14]

William James, while acknowledging that his
father credits Swedenborg with being the source of
his opinions, himself speaks of his father as 'an original thinker, whose philosophy was underived. Many
disciples of Swedenborg, wielding high authority,
say there is no warrant in the master's pages for
Mr James's views. It is certain, to say the very least,
that Mr James has given to the various elements in
Swedenborg's teaching an extremely different ac-
centuation and perspective relation to each other, from
anything other readers have been able to find.' [15]

A very intelligent disciple, Miss Kellogg, holds
that James 'bases his philosophy upon ideas derived
from Swedenborg, but the philosophy itself comes
not from Swedenborg: it is profoundly original.' [16]

The 'secret of Swedenborg' remains as obscure as
the 'figure in the carpet.' Every great thinker, from
Plato down, has given occasion for a multitude of
schools. What is the *true* Platonism: that of Aristotle

(in his *Metaphysics*), or of the Platonic Academies, or of Plotinus, or of Pater, or of Paul Elmer More, or of Santayana? To pass beyond verbal repetition of the master's phrases to even the simplest sort of exposition involves interpretation—how much more when the disciple possesses parts and powers of his own, and wants not to repeat but develop. To such thoughtful disciples some parts of the master's thought and work seem more significant than others, to constitute his real contribution; these they would develop.

III

A view of Swedenborg very different from that of James was taken by the majority of those who professed his name. Swedenborg himself established no church; but English believers in his doctrines began to organize as early as 1778, and the first American New-Church society goes back to 1792.[17] At the time of Mr James' conversion, the Church of the New Jerusalem (as the Swedenborgian body is called) had already attracted much attention and gained considerable following among the educated and refined. In 1842 there were Swedenborgians in all states of the Union, said to amount to some five thousand in all.[18] They were equipped with clergy and publications—of which the *New Jerusalem Magazine* was chief; and they carried on extensive lecturing and propagandizing.

The years 1835 to 1850 may be taken as the period

during which Swedenborg and the New Church attracted most general attention and exerted most general influence. The period was that of the first great American *Aufklärung,* Transcendentalism. The Transcendental Club began its session in 1836; the *Dial* in 1840. Emerson's *Nature* appeared in 1836, his Divinity School address in 1838, the two volumes of his *Essays* in 1841 and 1844. In 1841 Theodore Parker preached his catastrophic sermon on 'the transient and the permanent in Christianity.'

Under the impetus of a kind of universal liberalism, 'emancipated' people looked tolerantly upon all sorts of novel doctrines and cults, optimistically hopeful that there was 'something in' all of them. Phrenology, mesmerism, hypnotic healing, spiritualism: all received respectful hearing during these years. In medicine, Hahnemann and Homeopathy were the choice of the forward-looking.[19] In the spheres of political and economic theory, the socialisms of St Simon, Robert Owen, and, above all, Fourier seemed to promise the speedy advent of a new and consummating Day.

Swedenborgianism palpably profited by this attitude of tolerance, inquiry, experiment. Its novelties and its sweeping claims, which in other days might suffice to dismiss it to obscurity, then afforded no presumption of its failure. Panaceas were the accepted thing; great, rather than modest, expectations the mark of genius as of truth.

Interest in Swedenborg was gereral among the

Transcendentalists, but Emerson did most to call the attention of the thoughtful. His lecture, 'Swedenborg, or the Mystic,' first delivered at Boston in 1845 and published, 1850, in *Representative Men,* mingled praise and censure, with, on the whole, a predominance of praise; and though the orthodox 'receivers' of the Heavenly Doctrines felt by no means satisfied with Emerson's account, his lecture introduced many to its subject, as it has continued to do.[20]

Others as well as Emerson were favorably impressed by the work of the Swedenborg Association of London, organised in 1845 for the publication of the scientific and philosophical works, with J. J. G. Wilkinson as its leading spirit. Wilkinson's editions of *The Animal Kingdom* and *The Economy of the Animal Kingdom,* with lengthy introductions, received Emerson's eulogy and won him Emerson's friendship.[21]

In America, the cause of the Swedenborgians gained not only from Emerson's endorsement, with however many qualifications attended, but, more directly, from the conversion to the faith of the Rev. George Bush, distinguished Hebrew scholar and professor at New York University, who, in 1845, came out openly in favor of the New Church, with a public lecture on 'The Future Life, according to the disclosures of Swedenborg.'[22]

Dr Bush's position and learning entitled him to the respect of the intellectual world; and his courses of lectures all over the East seem to have attracted much attention. The two principal attacks on Swedenborgianism confess their origin in the success of these lectures. Dr Leonard Woods, of the Andover Seminary, testifies in the preface to his *Lectures on Swedenborgianism* (1846), 'The writings of Swedenborg have been before the world for almost a century. But, until of late, they received only a very limited measure of attention from the Christian community, especially in this country. Within a short time, however, the public attention has, to a considerable extent, been turned to those writings by the lectures and publications of the Reverend George Bush. . . .'; and Dr Pond's *Swedenborgianism Examined* (1846) bears the same witness.[23]

Heraud, in his remarkably unpartisan essay on Swedenborg which appeared in 1841 and was almost certainly read by James, defines the two groups who read the seer: the separatists who took his writings as infallible; the idealists and men of letters who found him intellectually quickening. 'The majority, of course, accept Swedenborg as a prophet, whose inspirations are to substitute theirs. He has, however, some transcendental students who cite him only as an example of the perpetual possibility of inspiration; who, while they admit his, claim a similar privilege for themselves. . . . Our friend, Thomas Carlyle, would include him among his heroes who have obtained the world's worship; and one of the said Carlyle's own disciples in America (Mr Ralph Waldo Emerson) has claimed for Swedenborg particular consideration as a literary man.' Heraud adds that the Swedenborgians are 'chiefly very intellectual people. No wonder; for their master has perfectly succeeded in constructing a religion for the scientific man.' [24]

The vogue of Swedenborgianism meant a potential audience of some dimensions for James' writings; and his espousal of Swedenborgianism implied no such intellectual perversity or queerness, entailed no such loss of intellectual status, as it might today.

IV

But the members of the New Jerusalem Church were to take no real satisfaction in James' conversion; must rather have found his reputed advocacy of their doctrines an embarrassment to the cause. For James' Swedenborgianism was *sui generis*. Not only was he the life-long excoriator of the *soi-disant* New Jerusalem, as he was wont to call the Swedenborgian organization; not only did he refuse to attribute inerrancy to Swedenborg's revelations; but his whole exposition of Swedenborg differed, almost *toto coelo*, from that of the New Church.

Mr James regarded the New Churchmen of his day as literalists, who thought to do Swedenborg homage by quoting his *ipsissima verba* instead of comprehending his doctrine and then developing and applying it. To James, this was doing his mentor a distinct disservice. Swedenborg, like every other great teacher, was by no means of a piece, by no means evenly significant. His doctrines must be studied as proceeding from a central point of view; and it was the point of view rather than the details of the system which really counted.

'In Swedenborg, as in other writers, much must count for *slag,* and the question "what is the *real* Swedenborg," will naturally be solved by different students in different ways.'[25] James would have admitted that. But he would insist that no mere study of Swedenborg would do, no mere assiduity of reading. Swedenborg must be interpreted; and one must read him, not pedantically but largely, with imagination and philosophic perception.

We are to abstract our thoughts from time, space, and persons when we essay spiritual reflection, James learns from Swedenborg; and he accuses the members of the *soi-disant* New Jerusalem of failing to follow Swedenborg's advice. The consequence is a philosophy wrested into an ecclesiasticism.

The principal doctrines of Swedenborg as interpreted by the New Church concern the Lord, the Word, and the Future life. Rejecting a trinity of persons, Swedenborg substitutes a modalistic trinity (Love, Wisdom, and Power). These essences subsist in a personal God, Jehovah-Jesus. God Himself descended to earth in the Incarnation, not a subsidiary deity: Jesus Christ is the only God.

The Holy Scriptures owe their divinity and inerrancy not to their letter, which is accommodated to

the understanding of men and hence fallible, but
to their 'inner sense,' which uses the literal sense as
its basis and containant and is united to it by exact
correspondence. *Allegory* and *symbolism* suggest
themselves to the reader of patristic and mediaeval
exegesis as the appropriate terms in which to describe
Swedenborg's interpretation of the Scriptures. But
New Churchmen reject the terms as inaccurate: Swedenborg did not mean that the human fancy might
find play in detecting pleasing analogies and parabolic
refinements, but that within the letter of the Word
there really exists a continuous inner meaning, dealing always not with history and geography and persons but with spiritual states.

Swedenborg teaches the existence of three states
after death, a temporary and provisional intermedi-
ate world of spirits, and a heaven and a hell, both
tripartite and both eternal. New Churchmen stress as
their teacher's contribution to Christian thought of
the after life his rejection of what may be called
its topography. Heaven and hell are states, not places,
asserts Swedenborg; and he denies in consequence
the physical torments of the orthodox hell.

After death, the souls of men go directly into the
world of spirits. Swedenborg denies the resurrection
of the body, and holds that the Last Judgment, dated
by such Christians as repose any literal belief in it,
at the 'end of the world,' occurred in the spiritual
sphere, before his own eyes, in 1757. The Second
Advent of the Lord is a coming, not in person, but

in the Word. The opening by Swedenborg's books, especially the *Arcana Coelestia,* of the Inner Sense of the Word, constitutes the Second Coming.[26]

Swedenborg himself founded no ecclesiasticism. He published his voluminous expositions of Scripture and his theological treatises at his own expense, and sent copies to the bishops and scholars of Europe, seeming not to doubt that the Divine Providence would open the eyes of these spiritual leaders in high places, and that through their mediation the New Church, the Lord's Final Dispensation, would descend to earth.[27]

In this hope he was, of course, naïvely sanguine. A few Lutheran and Anglican clergymen, notably the Rev. John Clowes and the Rev. Augustus Clissold, preached the doctrines of Swedenborg without seceding from the Established Church; a few laymen, notably Wilkinson and Tulk, did the same.[28] And to this day, there remains a handful of receivers of Swedenborgianism within orthodox communions. But in the main Swedenborg now speaks through a church, with its own clergy, orders, and sacraments.

V

It was from this ecclesiastical organization purporting to be the New Church that James principally dissented and against which he protested with all his vehemence; for he believed the New Church a spirit which was first to permeate and then to dissolve all existing ecclesiasticisms. But from the *doctrines* held by the organization he really differed quite as radically. For all his philosophy and symbolism, Swedenborg was susceptible of a supernaturalistic, quasi-orthodox reading. If he denied the Trinity, it was upon opposite grounds to the Socinian denial—from a kind of super-orthodoxy. And for all his insistence that miracles have a point and a meaning beyond the display of power, Swedenborg seems not to have doubted that the miracles really occurred. And though technically a heretic, Swedenborg took his theology with the utmost seriousness, formulated it with the utmost precision, and inveighed with the utmost earnestness against other theologies.

But James was in no sense a literalist. He tells us that he holds to the Virgin Birth,[29] but it may very well have been in some very special or Pickwickian sense. He found controversy over the *facts* of the Bible irritating and a weariness to the flesh; and when pressed by some earnest inquirer to state what *facts* he believed he was always impatient to get back to *meanings*. 'I don't at all see,' he says, 'how men can set any intellectual value upon the literal facts ascribed to Christ by his disciples and followers in the flesh: such as his birth from a woman who had never carnally known a man, and his resurrection from death in his own natural body. For these facts are hopelessly miraculous, and miracles pointedly disown intellectual appreciation in appealing to the profounder, more sincere and affectionate homage of

the heart. Accordingly I am not at all inclined to
rate too high the intellectual worth of the tedious,
unprofitable, and dishonest controversy which our
deceased Christian church still manages to keep up
with science or common sense over the alleged miraculous facts of Christ's birth, death, and resurrection.' [80]

The Incarnation is pointless viewed, as Swedenborgians and orthodox alike view it, as an isolated conjunction of God and man. 'Common sense takes no
account of any strictly personal or individual experiences in men, save in so far as these experiences profess
to be a simple foreshadowing of yet unknown and
majestic *race*-possibilities.' To James, 'Christ's birth,
death and resurrection would have done little good
to mankind, if they had not been essentially metaphysical or *apocalyptic* facts, designed to shed light upon
the *universal* relations of man to God, and of God to
man. . . .' [81] The Incarnation, or God's descent into
the body of humanity, but began in Jesus and is destined to go on until every last son of man is spontaneously the lover of God in his fellows. The Lord
of whom Swedenborg speaks, and whom Swedenborgians have identified with the historic Jesus, the
Lord in whom the invisible God is incarnate—this
Lord is that Man of Destiny, that *Maximus Homo,*
of which the historic Jesus was the foreshadowing and
the type.

The Swedenborgians, even Wilkinson, the only
man to whom James could address himself at all
intelligibly, made much of the doctrine of the Lord's

Glorification; but by it they meant an historical oc-
currence. James writes Wilkinson: 'You Swedenborgians are wont to talk of the glorification of the human
nature in the Christ, as of certain phenomena which
transpired within the *spatial* limits of Christ's body,
and remain permanently confined to those limits
throughout eternity, thus practically turning the
Christ into a mere miracle, or Divine *tour de force,*
fit for Barnum's museum of curiosities. . . . To the
spiritual apprehension the Lord is not a finite historical person capable of being outwardly discrim-
inated from other persons: He is the infinite Divine
love and wisdom in union with every soul of man.
*He has no existence or personality apart from such
union.'*

'When I think spiritually of the Christian truth, I
do not think of Jesus personally, except as it were to
anchor or define my thought. I think quite away
from Him personally indeed, and fix my attention
upon what is universal to man. . . .' The life and
death and *glorification* of the Christ 'spiritually im-
ply, that *infinite love and wisdom constitute the inmost and inseparable life of man, and will ultimately
vindicate their creative presence and power by bringing the most degraded and contemned forms of humanity into rapturous conscious conjunction with
them.'* [32]

All this thoroughly distressed Wilkinson, who,
independent and liberal though he was, held staunchly
to the traditional view of the Incarnation. 'I cleave

to the historical,' he writes, 'as a Romanist to his dolls; and when you talk of *the* Christ, I feel pained at the definite article, because it makes Christ Himself—the only one I know—indefinite. . . .' Or, as he writes a year later, 'I think you scientifically wrong in evaporating the personality of Christ in order to procure the universality of *the* Christ. . . . You seem to think that the human existence of Christ is not his Divine Existence also. . . .'[33]

Mr James persists. 'Personal adulation of the Christian name,' homage to the *person* of Jesus, is a 'complete waste of breath'; and much that passes for Christian worship is a 'mere mercenary mummery.' 'The worshipper of God at this day knows Christ no longer after the flesh but only after the spirit. . . .' 'In this broadening spiritual daybreak that surrounds us, the break of God's true, all-embracing, or universal day, a day therefore which shall never know night— it is to the last degree unmanly to persist in calling Christ lord! lord! no matter in what tuneful or melodious fashion, under the silly impression that some paltry advantage may accrue thereby to our own petty souls.'[34]

And what of Swedenborg's celebrated doctrine of *correspondence*? Its principle found ready acceptance; and James testifies that 'men of the profoundest scientific culture'—such men, that is, as Swedenborg, Fourier, Emerson, Garth Wilkinson, Sampson Reed, C. A. Tulk—'do not hesitate to assume the existence of an exact correspondence between man spiritually

viewed, viewed in his affections or passions and his intellect on the one side, and the entire phenomena of
the visible universe on the other.' [35] That the natural
world was effect and not cause of the spiritual world
he profoundly believed. But he never busied himself
with puzzling out the 'continuous inner sense' of the
Word, and rarely makes specific use of the 'science
of correspondences.' Those 'who are curious in the
symbolism of the sacred writings may like to know
that this finite or natural selfhood of man is what is
represented, according to Swedenborg, by the Eve
of the garden of Eden. The sensual principle and its
necessary power in the infantile development of man,
is what is symbolized by the serpent, and his influence
with Eve,' [36] he informs us in a footnote to *Miscellanies;*
and in his later works the significance of Adam and
Eve finds frequent place. Beyond this he scarcely
goes.

And the 'spiritual world.' Popular opinion has it—
so far as there is a 'popular opinion' of them—that
Swedenborgians are a very refined and cultivated and
'dreamy' people who indulge in mystical experiences
and think much about heaven and the dead. 'Oh yes,'
someone says, 'I once knew some Swedenborgian
ladies—very charming people they were, too. At table,
they always set a place for their father, who died
twenty years ago. I used to think that such a *sweet*
custom.'

One can hear Mr James snort at the informer.
Swedenborg was the least 'dreamy' person one can

imagine, the most bolt upright and wide awake and matter of fact and drily precise. And his *Heaven and Hell,* albeit in apocalyptic guise, sets forth the principles which operate in the world of men and determine that character, which is destiny, here and now. And Swedenborg's religion crowns not contemplation and rapture but action and use. 'The life of religion is to do good.'[37]

If Swedenborg's books have comforted the bereaved (as doubtless they have), that is well and good. And it is well that *ex auditis et visitis* the states of 'post-mortem existence' should be exhibited as exactly correspondent to life on earth, so that no slightest miraculous jugglery or hocus pocus, but only a man's nature, can assign his abode, which is his state; in consequence of which all further curiosity upon the subject will cease, and men will turn from empty speculations and idle fancies to that reality which alone constitutes this world or that to come. But Swedenborg's manly soul must not be confounded with those who inquire of spirits that peep and mutter. He speaks not of the dead but of the living.

'Our eternal interests are of course the only real ones; but these are the interests of our true manhood, and have therefore no more relevancy to the life beyond the grave than they have to that now present. They have no relevancy to time or space whatever, but only to the habitual and cultivated temper of our own minds, whether it be one of living conformity to the Divine spirit or of merely professed conformity. . . .

We are greatly mistaken in supposing that the life which Christ reveals, God's true life in man, is mere *post-mortem* existence, or has any particular respect to the literal extension of the personal consciousness beyond the grave.'[88]

'I have no doubt indeed that I shall live after death. . . . But any amount of mere post-mortem consciousness would prove a sorry equivalent for immortality.'

And how do I win this immortality? Through belief in Jesus; through a righteous life? Not at all. *Sell all that thou hast* (all your personal pretensions to goodness or heaven) *and give to the poor*. Or, as James puts it, 'a man realizes his life Divine and immortal only by coming to view himself as so much mere rubbish in comparison with his fellows, and clinging with renewed affections to his Divinely redeemed race or nature.'

James parted company with both the Swedenborgians and the orthodox in his insistence that the *letter killeth*. Neither 'my faith nor my reason,' he writes towards the end of his life, 'is at all disconcerted by the current rationalistic criticism of the gospels.' He watched the intellect of Church expended in the defense of the Bible miracles, and wondered why men could not distinguish between *facts* and *truths*. The truths of religion do not rest upon the evidence of the senses; and the church can cheerfully entrust the province of the senses, and whatever is alleged to have happened within it, to science; assured that the truths which God has *revealed to the heart* can receive neither corroboration nor contradiction from science.[39]

In consequence of Mr James' audacious views he was a truant from church and spiritually quite isolated; and in this position he remained all his life.

VI

His *Letter to a Swedenborgian,* published in 1847, sufficiently defines his attitude toward the Church. In this early book, he asserts that the Church of Christ is not an Ecclesiasticism; and he but reorchestrates his theme in the later tract which wears its thesis as title.

The *Letter* and the *Church of Christ* (1854) both reveal James as particularly vehement against the Swedenborgians. This, of course, follows from his assumption that they, at least, ought to know better. Other ecclesiasticisms may placidly go on supposing God gratified by sacrifice and burnt-offering; not so the Swedenborgians.

While the orthodox Swedenborgians interpreted their seer as asserting that the Last Judgment had terminated the older ecclesiasticisms, Roman Catholic and Reformed, only to introduce a new ecclesiasticism, with its distinctive doctrines, clergy, and sacraments, James held that the New Church of which Swedenborg spoke differed *toto coelo* from any earlier 'church': having hitherto tabernacled in representative rites and ceremonies, the Divine was now to seek direct entrance into men's hearts and men's social relations.

In his *Letter* James considers the history of Christendom. To Swedenborg and his contemporaries, he asserts with much justice, the church was 'still a civil institution, intimately blended with the political life of the nations, and by no means, as now, the mere nursery of a self-involved pietism. . . . EVANGELICAL RELIGION, as it is termed, (*quasi lucus a non lucendo,*) had not then risen with its tests of "inward experience," to divide Christendom into "the church" and "the world"; and the mass of the people apparently still believed that to do justice, to love mercy, and to walk humbly before God, were the sum of the Christian life.' [40]

To-day, says James, to-day in America, our notions of the church are bare and meager. We identify it with public worship and with the propagation thereby of a personal and private intimacy with God. 'It is a thing as much divorced from the ordinary interests and life of humanity . . . as the institution of Freemasonry, being wholly set apart to the advocacy of our interests beyond the grave.' The American church of James' day preached no hint of the 'social gospel.' 'As at present constituted it is the citadel and shield of individualism, or the selfish principle. . . . It wholly ignores all questions of political and social reform, or if it does recognize them at all, it is only to stigmatize their gathering urgency with the name of "infidelity." ' [41]

Of this sort of 'church' Swedenborg had no experience and no notion. He had no desire to substitute a

new sort of public worship for an old, a novel set of
dogmas for an accustomed. By the 'end of the church'
Swedenborg meant the end of the whole earlier ecclesiastical and political and economic dispensation—
the end of what Whitman called feudalism and Fourier (and sometimes James after him) civilization. By
the Christian Church Swedenborg meant *the constituted social order of Christendom* . . . ; he meant
the public order of Christendom, based upon the principle of an hereditary aristocracy, and involving the
whole framework of society—involving the enforced
subjection of the peasant to the peer, of the laity to
the clergy, of the slave to the master, of the ignorant
to the learned.' [42]

It is the church thus broadly interpreted which
Swedenborg regards as having come to an end to be
superseded by a New Church, a new social and spiritual
order. And in the American republic James finds
confirmation of this view. Here is a nation without
either feudal aristocracy or established church and
priesthood. 'The people of this land earnestly seeking
to rescue the freest development of their human faculties, and the highest possible enjoyment of life, did
not feel the established institutions of Christendom
to be necessary to that end, and they made no provision for them in their polity.' [43]

It was in the gradual extinction of charity, brotherly
love, that Swedenborg saw the infallible token of the
end of the church. Piety, too, had waned, though
Christendom was by no means devoid of it. Sweden-

borg differed from such of his contemporaries as felt
alarm over the spiritual state of Europe in not supposing that more religiosity was the remedy, more
fervid confessions of sin, more histrionic conversions,
more *personal* piety. Wesley and Whitefield and Edwards 'too deplored the evils of Christendom, but they
thought the true panacea lay in the increase of its
piety. They set about an agitation to this effect, and
accomplished it to some extent.'

The result, James judges, has scarcely been to im-
prove the general life of men in Christendom. The
peculiarity of 'evangelical religion,' he says bluntly,
is 'to deaden men's sympathies for the actual and
present ills of humanity, in favor of their possible
future ills; and so to neutralize much of the energy
which would otherwise have been available for the
mitigation of human suffering. . . . It is essentially
anti-social. It cares only for its own soul. The ameli-
orating progress of science accordingly in late years
has met with nothing but obstruction from the progress of so-called "evangelical religion." They are in
fact the antagonist influences of the day.' [44]

Of course the Oxford Movement comes off no better than the Evangelical Revival. Newman and Pusey,
no more than Wesley or Edwards, concerned themselves with the social gospel. 'Swedenborg was bound
to reject piety [the Evangelical panacea] therefore as
the all-sufficient remedy for the evils of Christendom.
Still less sympathy, if that were possible, had he with
the Romish error, now becoming English also, of the

Church being constituted by the Word and its sacraments.' [45]

But what of the New Jerusalem Church? Is this
the New Church of which Swedenborg speaks?
James' answer is of course obvious. The New Church
of which Swedenborg speaks is not an ecclesiasticism
at all, however improved over old models.

'Swedenborg looked upon sectarianism or separatism
as a crying evil of Christendom. He thought that a
difference of opinion on doctrinal subjects, ought never
to divide those who were intent on reducing the divine commandments to life. . . . According to Swedenborg . . . the new economy was to supervene not
as a new and visible sect, but as a spirit of freedom
and rationality in the old sects. It HAS come, or
rather is now coming, as a spirit of Love among all
the sects, flinging a veil of obscurity over those ob-
trusive doctrinals, whose fruit has always been dis-
union, and bringing into light those hidden charities
whose only possible issue is peace.' [46]

The professed followers of Swedenborg are intent
upon narrowing the sweep of Christ's Church while
the whole tendency of the times is to broaden it to the
full compass of humanity. While 'New Churchmen'
rebaptize their converts and practise close communion
in the privacy of some inner room, [47] James urges that
the sacraments should be lifted 'out of their old, limited, and no longer rational function, which is that of
separating Christian from Pagan, into their new, universal, and worthy application, which is that of uniting

all good men without respect to their formal religious differences, in one divine brotherhood.' The true Church of Christ, 'as Swedenborg shows, has ever been coextensive with the human race. Whosoever lives a life of charity—I do not mean a life of alms-giving, nor a technically devout life, but a really humane life, by the conscientious avoidance of whatever wrongs the neighbor—is *ipso facto* a member of that church, though he himself have never heard the name of Christ. In a word true humanity constitutes the Church of Christ, and everything else is "mere leather and prunella." ' [48]

A review of the *Letter* in the socialist journal, the *Harbinger*, remarks, quite justly, 'There is a most manifestly "Associative" tendency in this whole essay on the church. It is Fourierism in the sense which alone does justice to the thought of Fourier. It does not postpone the true life of man into another world; it does not deal with mere theology, but seeks to make the actual present life religious, and to give a social body to Christianity.' [49]

The name of Fourier does not occur in the *Letter*, it is true; and James proffers no method for bringing about the desired state of things: 'How this new condition of things is to be actualized, is a question which I do not propose to discuss with you.' But 'Associative' in his outlook James surely is; and with Fourier he contemplates the approaching end of a negative morality, the cessation of all dualisms between instinct and conscience, the flesh and the spirit, self-love and social.

The 'titular church' affirms that 'self-denial is the essence of virtue; that men *can not* be good without it; and that any attempt of the Divine consequently to institute a virtuous progeny on the earth, a progeny in whom interest and duty, pleasure and conscience, shall perfectly harmonize, and prompt to like issues, must necessarily prove fallacious.'[50] That 'all the actual virtue of our past history has involved self-denial,' James, in the name of the New Church of all humanity, does not deny. But he refuses to rest in any such conception of virtue as anything more than temporary. The celestial men of Swedenborg's prehistoric church felt no conflict between desire and duty. The men of the New Age will effect, in the Divine Providence, a union of desire and duty, not retrospective or imitative, and not supermundane: the kingdoms of this earth are presently to be made the kingdoms of our God.

CHAPTER V

FOURIER

....

I

JAMES' first acknowledged publication, his *What Constitutes the State*, indicated clearly enough the direction of his thoughts, adumbrated the particular blend of religion with sociology which was to be his. The little book, an expansion of a lecture delivered before the Young Men's Association in Albany in December, 1845, found for itself extended and favorable review in the *Harbinger*, then published at Brook Farm. Mr James is declared 'a thinker, and not a mere repeater of the ideas of other men'; he is highly complimented upon his philanthropic spirit. Clearly he is working in the direction of Association. But he falls short in limiting himself to social theory, suggesting no method for attaining his ends.[1]

In an age so prone to methods of social salvation, Mr James' reluctance to prescribe must have seemed, indeed, perverse. He does, it is true, declare the state of man 'an associate state';[2] but he otherwise uses no terms at all redolent of party. James' purpose, in this early and rather diffuse essay, was to associate religion with men's present and social life, disengaging it from its purely theological, eschatological preoccupations; similarly, to interpret the State as consisting in the social relationships which men sustain one to another rather than in forms of government.

He reminds us that 'if the State really stood in the political forms of society, then treason to the State would always be opposition to the government. In which case our forefathers would have been traitors to Great Britain. . . .'[3] But most men can distinguish Law from laws, and are capable of a provisional loyalty to the latter quite compatible with abiding loyalty to the former. In every government, there are some features which spring from expediency rather than absolute justice; but 'so long as government does not claim infallibility to its policy, but allows it to be gradually shaped by the advancing life of humanity,' we can obey it as an expression of the State.[4]

The true State, however, is nothing short of the whole human society without respect to race or nation. 'THE STATE then means simply the social condition peculiar to man: a condition which makes his highest life to depend upon his relations to his fellows, or which limits his enjoyment of life within the limits of his love to his brother.'[5]

This social or moral (in this lecture, contrarily to his later practise, James uses these terms as synonymous) nature of man, which distinguishes him from

the animals, is due neither to the necessities of man's
natural existence nor to his volition. Man's social obligations antecede choice: the 'social contract' is a
fiction; the hypothesis 'which makes the social State
the result of a voluntary compact, destroys the whole
ground of moral distinctions among men, by denying
the subordination of the individual to society, and pronounces the words virtue and vice to be empty sounds,
signifying nothing.'⁶

No, man's conscience, through which speaks his ob-
ligation to his neighbor, is not to be dissolved into its
constituents; it is a primary, undeniable element of
man's nature. It is the living testimony to the reality
of the State as consisting in the unity of man's being,
'his essential or creative unity, the unity of being
which all men have in God the Creator.' The social
conscience is 'an *instinct*. It lies deeper than the foundations of my understanding, it lies entirely behind
my will; and I can only explain it by saying, that it
is a prompting of the divine spirit within me, *to deny
which would be sin;* would be a virtual abnegation of
my filial relation to Him.'⁷

The reality of the social conscience consists in its
reflection of the Divine Love: 'It is by virtue of this,
their universal unity of being in divine Love, that men
are rendered equally dependent upon their social relations . . . for the highest development of life.' And
the permanence of the State consists in its expression
of the very nature of God: 'if the being of man lay in
anything but divine Love, that is to say, if his Creator

were anything else than perfect Love, then the *social* state of man would proportionately disappear, and the tendency would be towards the individual and solitary life, instead of the social and united one.' [8]

Having vindicated the essentially spiritual origin and constitution of the State, James now turns to a brief enunciation of the other half of his thesis, the essentially social character of true spirituality. 'Goodness, it will be admitted, is only another name amongst men for use. The measure of a man's goodness is his use to society.' The evil man is he who 'performs *no* use to society, but seeks rather to make society subservient to him.' 'We may clothe ourselves with conventional sanctity as with a garment, we may experience all manner of convictions and conversions, we may rejoice in an apostolically-descended baptism to our hearts' content,' but we shall be judged only in respect to our justice and charity.' [9]

Nowhere among the present polities of the earth shall we find anything approaching a pure exhibition of the social State. But we must not doubt that 'this day is hastening on with all the speed wherewith divine Love can overcome the selfishness of man, and that our earth will yet surely reflect the splendors of the eternal State, and all the vices which now deform civilization disappear before a universal reverence for its great constitutive Law.' [10] The last three pages marshal, somewhat grandiloquently, the evidences of a new day for humanity: 'what a spectacle of progress does the last half-century present!' James' imagination fires at the achievements of the Nineteenth Century. 'The sciences, scorning any longer to be the mere sounding-boards of a professional or chartered vanity, have . . . proclaimed their true mission to be the practical melioration of our common life. Astronomy, chemistry, geology, have leaped from the ineffectual grasp of a bewildered pedantry, to summon all men alike to the banquet of wonders unfolding in the heavens above, and the earth beneath. Education, universal education, is the cry of advancing humanity throughout Christendom. . . . The drunkard, the pauper, the lunatic, the slave, lie no longer the victims of a cold indifference, but are laid each on the heart of his fellowman, and there warmed back into newness of life. War is becoming an increasing abomination to all humane hearts. . . .'

'Time would fail me to glance at a tithe of the outward proof of progress our eyes witness.' But some must be named, and we hear of 'our steamboats, our railroads, our magnetic telegraphs, which laugh to scorn the limitations of time and space'; in these, James sees 'the gigantic throbbings wherewith dumb nature herself confesses the descent of that divine and universal spirit, which even now yearns to embrace all earth's offspring in the bonds of a mutual knowledge and a mutual love.' [11]

II

The *Harbinger* was correct in the conviction that James shared its outlook in essentials. Upon his return to New York, he soon found himself attracted to a socialist movement then at its height; and though *What Constitutes the State* bears no evidence of his having read Fourier, James came presently—through the mediation of his old friend, Parke Godwin, doubtless [12]—to admire Fourier and to ally himself with the Associationists, as the disciples of Fourier were called.

The transition from Swedenborg to Fourier might then easily be effected. Upon one doctrine, at least, and that a cardinal one with the Swedenborgians, the philosophers saw eye to eye. Fourier also enunciated the great law of the correspondence between the spiritual and the natural, between the soul of man and kingdoms—animal, vegetable, and mineral—of this world. He held that the different kingdoms of Nature are, 'in all their details, so many mirrors of some effect of our passions: they form an immense museum of allegorical pictures in which are depicted the crimes and the virtues of Humanity.' [13] And so strongly was Fourier impressed with this law of Analogy, that he felt, his biographer tells us, an insurmountable aversion to some animals. 'Such was the caterpillar, emblem of Civilization, the filthy, voracious, devastating caterpillar, which is metamorphosed into the brilliant butterfly, as the impure and odious society it represents must be transformed into Harmony; such was also the spider, emblem of the civilized shopkeeper . . . ; Fourier could not see these hideous emblems of subversion without experiencing a disgust mingled with horror.' [14]

Fourier indeed had his views, always striking, often suggestive, sometimes merely fantastic, on all subjects. He offered a complete system of human knowledge— theology and psychology as well as economics and sociology, and even astronomy and geography curious in kind.[15] But his disciples, quite properly, estimated his social theory as his significant contribution; never attempted thorough-going defense of the whole range of his ideas; and were quite ready to concede theological and metaphysical supremacy to Swedenborg.

At least two 'phalanxes' owed their existence to Swedenborgians—those at Leraysville, Pennsylvania, and at Canton, Illinois;[16] but far more significant was the very generally accepted conjunction of the names of Swedenborg and Fourier as, jointly, the prophets of the New Age, one in the spiritual world, the other in the natural.

James' friend Godwin's *Popular View of the Doctrines of Charles Fourier* (1844), in a chapter on 'Universal Analogy,' points out the resemblance between Fourier's 'analogies' and Swedenborg's 'correspondences,' observing that between Swedenborg's 'revelations, in the sphere of spiritual knowledge, and Fourier's discoveries in the sphere of science, there has been remarked the most exact and wonderful coincidence. . . .' 'These two great minds,' he continues,—'the greatest beyond all comparison in our later days,—were the instruments of Providence in bringing to light the mysteries of His Word and Works . . . It is no exaggeration, we think, to say that they are THE TWO commissioned by the Great Leader of the Christian Israel, to spy out the Promised Land of Peace and Blessedness.' [17]

Between thirty and forty articles on Swedenborg and Swedenborgian subjects appeared in the *Harbinger*. Yet most of the Fourierists who eulogized Swedenborg were not New Churchmen: Godwin, John S. Dwight, and Charles A. Dana, all copious contributors to the *Harbinger* and all given to associating the names of the two great prophets, none of them adhered to the denomination. [18]

Swedenborg, says Dwight, 'we reverence for the greatness of his thought. We study him continually for the light he sheds on so many problems of human destiny, and more especially for the remarkable correspondence, as of inner with outer, which his revelations present with the discoveries of Fourier concerning social organization, or the outward forms of life. The one is the great poet and high-priest, the other the great economist, as it were, of the harmonic order, which all things are preparing.' 'In religion we have Swedenborg; in social economy Fourier; in music Beethoven."

Dana joins the names of Swedenborg, Fourier, and Goethe. 'In these three eminent persons is summed up the great movement towards unity in universality, in religion, science and art, which comprises the whole domain of human activity.'

George Ripley speaks of the 'sublime visions of the illustrious Swedish seer,' his 'bold poetic revelations,' his 'profound, living, electric principles,' the 'piercing truth of his productions.'

In England, Hugh Doherty, editor of the London Fourierist organ, the *Phalanx,* was a Swedenborgian of an eclectic sort, whom J. J. G. Wilkinson characterized as 'marrying Fourier to the New Church, giving the former, however, the masculine character in the compact.'[19] Wilkinson himself, for a period from 1846 on, lent himself to the union. He wrote a friend, likely James, 'All you say of the Association movement I echo from my heart. It is the morning brightness of the world's day.' Wilkinson's brilliant essay on 'Correspondences,' which appeared in Miss Elizabeth Peabody's symposium, *Aesthetic Papers,* was not, the author assured James, to sink into the 'mere laudation of Swedenborg,' but to 'prepare some to carry forward the views of Swedenborg and Fourier. . . .'[20]

In 1848, Dr Charles Julius Hempel of New York published, anonymously, a book which attracted much attention among both Associationists and New Churchmen—*The True Organization of the New Church as Indicated in the Writings of Emanuel Swedenborg and Demonstrated by Charles Fourier.*

Orthodox New Churchmen found the book exceedingly annoying. From their point of view its reading of Swedenborg was thoroughly faulty, especially on fundamentals. Hempel makes Swedenborg 'teach, or appear to teach, that self-love is the pivotal or fundamental love of all in the heavens.' He has read Swedenborg 'without having formed the most distant conception that he teaches the doctrine of regeneration, or that there is or can be any such thing.' Fourier believes that 'we have only to alter the external condition of men—place them in true relations to each other externally—bring them together into the Phalanx and arrange them in groups and series, and man is regenerated.'[21] Such a view, Bush and Reed, Hempel's reviewers, held, was surely far from Swedenborg's belief in the depravity of man and the necessity for regeneration.

The New Churchmen were not perhaps likely to be pleased with a work so condescending in its attitude to their body. Hempel declares them 'too full of the *pride of faith,* too contemptuous of whatever does not chime in with their man-worship of Swedenborg, too heedless of the deep and stirring emotions of living charity, ever to impress the world more than they have heretofore done, with the sublime truths revealed in the writings of Swedenborg.' They have reduced their doctrines to 'mere formulas of individual moralization, whereas they are universal principles, whose *true* application to the individual is only possible incidentally by using them as a foundation for the unitary organization of Society.'[22]

A far more favorable view of the book was taken by the Fourierites and their organ, the *Harbinger,* which published copious extracts from its pages.[23]

The doctrines of Fourier began first to be preached in America by Albert Brisbane, whose *Social Destiny of Man* appeared in 1840. Half extracts from Fourier, half commentary and application to the American scene, the book had an immense success. It converted to the cause, among others, Horace Greeley, then editor of the *New Yorker*. Two years later, after Greeley had founded the *Tribune* and it had attained a circulation exceeding 20,000, Brisbane began to contribute a column, at first twice a week, then three times a week, and later daily. Upon its first appearance, in 1842, the column bore the caption: 'ASSOCIATION; OR PRINCIPLES OF A TRUE ORGANIZATION OF SOCIETY. This column has been purchased by the Advocates of Association [Fourierism], in order to lay their principles before the public. Its editorship is entirely distinct from that of the *Tribune*.' In 1843, Brisbane established an independent monthly, *The Phalanx*, edited by himself and Osborne Macdaniel.[24]

After Greeley and Brisbane, the most influential of American Fourierists was James' friend, Parke Godwin, associate editor of the *Evening Post* and son-in-law of its editor-in-chief, William Cullen Bryant. His tracts, *Democracy, Constructive and Pacific* (1843) and *Popular View of the Doctrines of Charles Fourier* (1844), were effective and influential.

Brook Farm, most illustrious of American communities, 'went Fourierist' in 1844; in 1845 it began to publish the *Harbinger*, principal literary remains of the movement. George Ripley, Charles A. Dana, and John S. Dwight presided over the destinies of the new journal. Their prospectus announced: 'The principles of universal unity as taught by Charles Fourier, in their application to society, we believe are at the foundation of all genuine social progress. . . . While we bow to no man as an authoritative, infallible master, we revere the genius of Fourier too highly not to accept with joyful welcome the light which he has shed on the most intricate problems of human destiny.' [25]

The year 1843 constituted, perhaps, the focal period of the movement; and around that year, or following it within the 'forties, there came into being in America some thirty-four communities—*phalanxes* as they were called—attempting in varying degrees to follow the doctrines of Fourier and meeting with varying degrees of practical success.[26]

III

What *was* the doctrine of Fourier? The master summed it up in the proposition inscribed on his tombstone in Paris: *attractions are proportionate to destinies*. Men have everywhere sought to create order by suppressing the instincts, by crushing liberty. And they have only succeeded in effecting lawlessness and sloth and misery. Destroy the institutions of civilization, uncheck the instincts, let every man follow his desires, and you will have a universe at once orderly and productive and happy.

Why has God given us our passions if not to follow them? If he exists, if he is good, if he is just, if he does not deceive us, then he has given us vigorous emotions

that we may give expression to them, and has provided a reason far less vigorous because its office is
strictly ancillary. 'The antinomy of reason and passion is an error. Reason must collaborate with the
passions. It must be the vigilant minister, but subordinate and submissive. It must clarify the passions
in their progress, define them to themselves, relate
them to their end, coördinate their efforts,—in a word,
serve them intelligently, not combat them, and much
less, which is absurd, pretend to conquer them.' [27]

Fourier does not essay the promulgation of new laws
of ethics and economics: from his point of view all the
errors and catastrophes of history have arisen from
human attempts at legislation. 'To *make* laws, would,
in his opinion, be an usurpation of the divine attributes. There is, according to Fourier, only one legis-
lator, HE who distributes the *attractions* to all created
beings.' Fourier merely stands apart from civilization,
an impartial observer, and discerns these laws. 'His
respect for the Supreme Intelligence does not permit
him to suppose that He can have distributed passions,
instincts and characters, without foreseeing a mode of
social relations in which all these forces would have a
useful, harmonic employment, and would contribute
to the good of the mass at the same time, that they
made the happiness of the individual.' [28]

The butcher, the baker, the candlestick-maker, the
priest, the physician, the painter, the farmer—all these
vocations make their appeal. There is no occupation
necessary to the welfare of society to which a sufficient

number of persons is not, naturally, attracted. And, on the other hand, there is no human instinct for which there may not be found some expression useful to society. Fourier seriously suggests that as children are fond of mud and dirt, the work of scavenging may be given over to them.[29]

Civilization, as Fourier calls the present Christian capitalistic regime, twists and contorts the natures of men. The way out of this bondage is through the organization of the society into phalanxes. With all the precision of a scientist or engineer, Fourier gives us the dimensions of the phalanx, describes its buildings, its employments, its recreations. The phalanx must be large enough to constitute a cross-section of humanity, affording examples of all the varieties of human experience. Within the bounds of this repertory, every one may follow his own bent, assured that by so doing he will fulfill God's destiny for him and serve his fellows. And since men like variety (*papillonage*), and have lesser and subordinate as well as *ruling* passions, the phalanx will allow of alternation of work, so that all a man's capacities may be utilized. At Brook Farm, this meant that Ripley and Hawthorne did manual labor as well as intellectual.

It is not only man's vocational attractions which must be obeyed. Men and women are variously endowed erotically. Some by nature elect virginity (these Fourier calls the *vestals*); some marry and remain unswervingly constant to their partners; some are faithful in their fashion, Cynara-like, but find themselves

also attracted, from time to time, by others; some
are naturally fickle and forever shifting attachments.
Fourier finds all of these types in existence and, instead of establishing a rule or norm, coolly asserts
the equal right of all. God, he thinks, has evidently
intended not one but many sorts of happiness; and
man must not concern himself about others, certainly
not attempt to coerce them into conformity to himself,
but follow the law of his own nature. In 'civilization,'
the 'man who experiences happiness in a fixed and
durable union, would compel every one else to follow
the same style of life. But why so, if they are so happy
in another way?'

The innocent surprise of the question must indeed
amuse. But the answer to the riddle of the universe
is so very clear to Fourier that he sweeps aside traditional answers as of little moment and cannot suppose them really taken seriously.

He carries his belief in the divinity of our passions
to the extent of finding appointed partners for all.
There are many tastes in love, but God has provided
for all. He 'could not have given to a minority among
old men a tender attachment to young women, without having endowed a certain minority among young
women with a preference which inclines them towards
old men.' [30]

Fourier did not expect or intend his disciples to
put his doctrine of love into immediate practise. His
interpreter, Hennequin, assures us that 'The erotic
customs described by Fourier will not be admissible in

an experimental Phalanx; they will be established only
when decency and respect for woman shall have become general among the masses, only when the previous organization of labor shall have assured the lot
of women and children, whose existence is now so
precarious.' [31] But these 'French' views of love (for
Fourier was sometimes partially excused on the ground
of his nationality) distressed most English and Americans, and were a constant source of embarrassment to
those who sought to put Fourier's economic and social system into operation, as were some passages in
Swedenborg's *Conjugial Love* to Anglo-Saxon disciples of that seer. In vain did the Fourierists protest,
and quite honestly, that they accepted only their teacher's economics: the distrust persisted.

IV

With the details of Fourier's elaborate system we
need not concern ourselves, for James did not concern himself with them. As with Swedenborg, so
with Fourier, James cared only for the grand principles; and he accepted or rejected details according
to his inclination. He joined company with Fourier for
his attack on civilization and his promise of a new
era to be based not upon *morality* but upon the spontaneous expression of human instincts.

James agrees with Fourier first of all in the fundamental doctrine that the instincts are God-given, to be
indulged and followed, not inhibited. 'Every appetite

and passion of man's nature is good and beautiful,
and destined to be fully enjoyed,' he enunciates in
'Democracy and its Issues,' 'and a scientific [*i.e.,* so-
cialistic] society or fellowship among men would en-
sure this result. . . .' Only bad management upon the
part of society allows the passions to go to waste.
'Remove, then, the existing bondage of humanity, remove those factitious restraints which keep appetite
and passion on the perpetual look out for escape, like
steam from an over-charged boiler, and their force
would instantly became conservative instead of de-
structive.' [32]

He agrees, too, that the harmony we want, and
which God intends, is effected not by imitation or
conformity or any other sort of unison, but by each
individual emitting his own characteristic note in his
own characteristic timbre. Like the negroes and the
gipsies, we shall improvise, to discover that we richly
blend.

Thus James enunciates this law of unity in diversity:
'Exactly in the degree in which these various elements
become freely asserted, will their unity be manifested,
will human society become perfected. . . . The harmony is grand or complete just in the degree that its
elemental notes are relatively various and distinct. . . .
So in human society, if each member be similar in
genius, in taste, in action, to every other, we have at
best a dismal monotony, a mere mush of mutual deference and apology. But if each is distinctively himself,
or sharply individualized from every other, then we

have a grand choral life hymning the infinite various graces of the divine unity.' [33]

A new social order will be far from erasing these congenital differences between men: there will disappear only the arbitrary distinctions conferred by inherited station and property. 'Every one when human society is ripe, will receive an outward homage exactly proportionate to the measure of his genius, or his capacity of ideal action.' [34]

Envy will cease, for the "source of envy is always arbitrary privilege. . . . You do not envy Jenny Lind her power of song; you only envy her the grasp it has given her upon the public attention, the independent social position it has achieved for her. . . .' Or we feel envy of the luxuries which inherited wealth can procure, or the education by which the rich may develop their tastes and their talents. In a socialistic order, a 'society scientifically arranged,' there will exist none of these arbitrary inequalities. 'That is to say, a true society would guarantee to every man, woman and child, for the whole term of his natural life, food, clothing, shelter, and the opportunities of an education adapted to his tastes; leaving all the *distinction* he might achieve to himself, to his own genius freely influencing the homage of his fellow-men.' [35]

Our present social institutions must go, for man's spiritual unity can find adequate expression only in 'the organization of the whole race in perfect fellowship, an organization not by human legislation, not by police, not by contention, but by God's legislation which is SCIENCE [socialism], and primarily by that method of science which has been termed *the law of the series,* and applied to human passions [by Fourier].' [36]

Their views of labor and property correspond in the main. James believes with Fourier that the difference between 'attractive industry' and the involuntary servitude of the so-called working classes lies not in any wholesale aversion toward activity which workmen cherish, but in the degree to which work is adapted to worker. When every man has been set to doing with all his might what, by the whole constitution of his nature, he craves to do, he *will ask no other blessedness;* and society will be the gainer. *Attractions are proportionate to destinies;* and there is no necessary occupation to which a sufficient number are not, by their natures, drawn. Of his admirable butler James remarks, 'It is not indeed a dignified thing to wait upon tables. There is no dignity in any labor which is constrained by one's necessities. But still no function exists so abject or servile as utterly to quench the divine or personal element in it.' [37] The butler may be, as this one is, an artist.

Our 'entire system of trade, as based upon what is called "unlimited competition," is a system of rapacity and robbery.' And before man 'can truly act or show forth the divine power within him, he must be in a condition of perfect outward freedom, or perfect insubjection to nature and society; all his natural wants must be supplied, and all social advantages must be open to him.' [38]

James agreed with Fourier that vice and crime were the consequences of our present social order, and would not survive its downfall. 'No man is evil save by the constraint of a vicious social form; [so] that the responsibility of all crime refers itself therefore not to the individual, but to society . . . Make society do its duties to the individual, and the individual will be sure to do his duties to society. . . . In order to do away accordingly with all evil, it [society] only needs to *purge itself,* that is, to put away those absurd and defective arrangements which now beget the very crimes they punish, and substitute instead those scientific methods which make all action virtuous, by reconciling the interests of every individual, with the interests of all men.' [39]

V

Most audaciously of all, he endorsed, in principle, Fourier's views upon love and marriage. James testifies, 'I am indeed unconscious of any *outward* motive to the maintenance of the views I advocate. I am unconscious in other words of any desire after greater passional liberty in any sphere, than the present constitution of society affords me. I have never that I remember brought myself either by look or word or deed into illicit relation with any woman, living or dead. . . . In short, I keep the law even while I despise its righteousness.' [40]

But in theory he speaks with Fourier and affects no horror at that part of the prophet's teaching. He ex-

pects a day to dawn 'when the sexual relations will
be regulated in every case by the private will of the
parties; when the reciprocal affection of a man and a
woman will furnish the sole and sufficient sanction of
their material converse. . . . Thus, if a man's or
woman's affections bind them to an exclusive alliance
all their days, the law will approve. If, on the contrary, they lead the subject to a varied alliance, the law
will equally approve.'

Increased liberty in love must not, it is true, be
proposed unless 'a superior social order, or an order
which is not based exclusively upon the family,' be
instituted. But 'If like Fourier he can eliminate a
social order which is founded upon a harmony of all
the primitive sentiments of man, [f]or an entire harmony of the passions, then *with reference to that social
condition,* he is not only justified in demanding liberty
in love, but he is actually bound to do so. For in an
harmonic state of society, every normal passion of the
human breast claims a free ultimation, that is, an equal
respect with every other passion.'

Marriage:—'I admit that marriage is a divine institution; but then it must also be admitted that its divinity
resides only in its use, and not in its form. . . .'[41]

James published anonymously in 1848 a translation
of Victor Hennequin's *Les amours au Phalanstère,*[42]
with a preface, stating that, though the American
Union of Associationists is concerned only with
Fourier's views upon the reorganization of industry,
the translator endorses Fourier's views upon the rela-

tions of the sexes as interpreted by Hennequin, and 'wishes to provoke the attention of honest minds to the truths involved in these views.' Promiscuity, defines James, 'denotes the intercourse which has taken place between man and woman, unsanctioned by any ties of the heart, or by the reciprocal personal preference of the parties. . . . But where this mutual preference does not exist, where the husband does not inspire the highest affection of the wife, nor the wife that of the husband, then their intercourse is truly promiscuous, being the intercourse of consenting bodies merely, and dissentient souls.' This involves the distinction between the legal marriage, whether ordained by church or state, and the marriage of the heart.

A review of *Love in the Phalanstery* which appeared in the N. Y. *Observer,* 'an influential and highly respectable religious newspaper . . . of the Presbyterian denomination,' aroused Mr James' wrath, and he indited to the *Harbinger* a lengthy letter of protest. This in turn was answered by a Swedenborgian clergyman, the Rev. A. E. Ford; and James and Ford went on filling the columns of the *Harbinger* till its finish with their respective views of love and marriage.[43]

Dr M. Edgeworth Lazarus' *Love vs. Marriage,*[44] a consistent and obviously noble-minded exposition of Fourier's doctrine of passional attraction, appeared in 1852, dedicated 'To the modest and the brave of either sex, who believe that God reveals to the instinct of each heart the laws which he destines it to obey, who

fear not to follow the magic clew of charm, but defy
the interference of all foreign powers.' Though the
author quotes Emerson's poetry and Swedenborg's
prose, both at length, and respectfully, Mr James'
inveterate contrariness, together with his sincere devotion to 'conjugial love,' led him to publish in the
N. Y. *Tribune* a caustic review of Lazarus, urging that
the Family, not the Individual, should be regarded as
the nucleus of society. Out of this there grew an ex-
change of letters between James and the Editor of the
Observer, and this spread to include Horace Greeley,
indicted by the *Observer* for allowing any open discussion of marriage, and Stephen Pearl Andrews,⁴⁵
one of the most amazing of all the amazing radicals
of the day.

Andrews brought out in 1853 a collection of the
letters on 'Love, Marriage and Divorce, and the Sovereignty of the Individual'—finding reason for the
book in Greeley's refusal to allow his own final replies
to appear in the *Tribune.* In this controversy, Andrews
exhibits more consistency and clarity than his associates, and the points at issue are best put in his sum-
maries.

Andrews represents 'free love'; Greeley, adherence
to the traditional views of marriage: no divorce except
for adultery, and 'But for the express words of Christ,
which seem to admit Adultery as a valid ground of
Divorce, we should stand distinctly on the Roman
Catholic ground of No Divorce except by Death.'⁴⁶
But what does Mr James represent?

It is difficult to pin him down. Greeley is too conservative for him, Andrews too radical. And both, too, are given to being simple of expression and concrete in application, whereas when one tries to corner James or press him for an example, he escapes into metaphysical subtleties.

James confesses to believing that divorce ought always to be possible, so that marriage might never rest upon legal constraint, but always upon spontaneous devotion of heart to heart. Yet consistently carried out, this would lead to 'free love,' or be indistinguishable from it. James' first retort is the taunt, unworthy of him, that advocates of free love prostitute *love* to *lust*.

But the real ground of what appears evasion and inconsistency in James was clearly analysed by Andrews. James sincerely believes in spontaneity and passional freedom, but with equal sincerity he supposes that once legal marriage were abolished or divorce made universally accessible, spiritual marriage, or the spontaneous expression of the *conjugial* instinct which joins mates for life, would take its place: in other words, marital faithfulness would be the rule without law. It is not, then, that he is opposed to marriage, 'that is, to the same course of life which legal marriage enacts in the form of law, but because [he thinks that] this last is not merely unnecessary but hurtful in securing that end. This theory [of James], so stated, comes pretty much to what is entertained in this age, more or less distinctly, by a good many persons transcendentally inclined, and whose views of prospective human improvement take no broader and more practical shape than that of *spiritualizing* whatsoever things, however stupid, which happen now to exist among us.'

Andrews neatly puts the difference between James and himself: 'He, "for his part," has no doubt that "constancy would speedily avouch itself as the *law* of the conjugal relations, in the absence of all legislation to enforce it." I, for my part, don't know that. . . . Mr James claims Freedom because, for his part, he believes that Freedom will lead people to act just in that way he personally thinks to be right. I, on the contrary, claim Freedom for all Men and all Women, for no such personal reason, but because they have an inalienable God-given Right, high as Heaven above all human legislation, to judge for themselves what it is moral and proper for them to do or abstain from doing; so long as they do not cast the burdens of their conduct on me.' [47]

VI

In November, 1847, the *Harbinger,* weekly organ of the Fourierists, transferred its publication from Brook Farm to New York.[48] At Brook Farm, George Ripley had been its chief editor; the issues subsequent to the transfer were edited by Parke Godwin, N. Y., James' friend of his Princeton days, assisted by C. A. Dana and G. Ripley in New York and W. H. Channing and J. S. Dwight in Boston.

Hepworth Dixon, that irrepressible journalist, introduces into his sensational *Spiritual Wives* the name of 'the Rev. Henry James, a Brook Farm enthusiast, who scandalized society by making a public confession of his call to the New Jerusalem, [and] filled many pages of the *Harbinger* with proofs that there is so little difference between Fourier and Swedenborg in practice, that a convert of one reformer may admit the other reformer's claims; since Fourier's Passional series (a pretty French name for Free Love) might be readily made to run alongside of Swedenborg's toleration of concubines. In fact, this reverend author, a man of very high gifts in scholarship and eloquence, declared himself on spiritual grounds in favor of a system of divorce, which is hardly to be distinguished from divorce at will.'[49]

The account blends fact with piquant fiction. Mr James' views upon love and marriage and divorce require no repetition: they doubtless admit of journalistic paraphrase to such effect as Dixon's; and they certainly filled many pages of the *Harbinger*. But James might justly protest against the gratuituous *reverend*. He never asserted the identity or even practical identity of the views upon sex of Swedenborg and Fourier; nor indeed did Dr Lazarus. And James correctly affirms of the Brook-Farmers: they were 'a community with which, while it existed, I was in no relation whatever, either of knowledge or sympathy.'[50]

James knew Ripley, the founder of Brook Farm, only after, at the end of the community, Ripley had taken refuge in New York, earning a meager living as editorial writer for Greeley's *Tribune*. James found himself in closer sympathy with Ripley than with Greeley, and felt only admiration for the angelic serenity with which he bore his disappointment. 'I never saw a person so faultless in personal behavior,' James bore witness long after: 'While living on nothing at all, he was as cheerful and uncomplaining as if he lived in the skies; he was the best man in the transcendental movement.'[51]

After the *Harbinger* was moved to New York, James contributed to it thirty-two essays and reviews and letters:[52] the *kinds* are scarcely distinguishable, since customarily the letter turns into essay or the essay assumes the flexible organization of the letter, and both letter and essay are often started in their course by something provocative their author has just been reading. He writes on parallels between Fourier and Swedenborg; he attacks the Swedenborgian sect and differs with its doctors; he writes on love and marriage; he discusses the laws of creation and the constitution of human nature; he reviews the tracts which infest the day.

Twice he descends with zest to the notice of belles-lettres, upon the appearance of yet more novels from the prolific pen of G. P. R. James, whose namesake it amused him to be.[53] I say *descends to belles-lettres:* the descent is never really accomplished. Mr James reads *Gowrie* as he reads *Vanity Fair*—for its matter, for its criticism of life. He pronounces upon his author:

'apart from his mere narrative skill [which to Mr James was indeed 'mere'], James is a grievous goose.' The novelist, in other words, is a child so soon as he thinks, and a child prig at that. 'The forcible feebleness of his style which puts you off with flippancy in the place of vivacity, the laughable inanity of his moral reflections, the dismal puerility of his humor, and the total absence of *vraisemblance* in his dialogue, have often been remarked, but we have never seen attention pointed to the prudish creature's indelicacy . . . a puritan indelicacy, or an indelicacy which grows out of an excessive straining after conventional refinement. Thus if his hero and heroine should have been represented as sitting hand in hand by candle light, and the light should suddenly have gone out, the statistical wretch will proceed to assure you that the lovers at once released hands and moved their chairs two feet apart.' [54]

W. H. Channing's short-lived *Spirit of the Age* published a few of James' things—notably an essay on 'Vanity Fair, or Becky Sharp,' in which, as one might imagine, the sinner is preferred to the prig, and a review of Blake's poems, of which James' friend, Wilkinson, served as first editor.[55]

Neither the *Harbinger* nor the *Spirit of the Age* seems completely to have satisfied James, for he proposed the commencement of yet another journal for the spread of the New Thought. Advertisements appeared in the *Harbinger*: the *New Times,* to be inaugurated on the first of January, 1848, is characterized as 'a new monthly periodical, for the discussion of the important social, philosophical, and religious questions, which especially agitate the present epoch. The *New Times* will bring to the discussion of these questions, the most catholic spirit, and the light of positive principles. It will aim to maintain in the social sphere, the essential and permanent interests of man; in philosophy, to discover and set forth the laws of order, which govern the spiritual as well as the natural universe; and in religion, to assert and illustrate the distinctive hope of [sic] christianity, which is the universal establishment of fraternal relations among men, and the dominion of the divine justice on earth.' [56]

Mr James is announced as editor in chief, with the aid of an impressive list of 'constant contributors': Ripley, Parke Godwin, C. A. Dana, Wilkinson, G. H. Calvert, B. F. Barrett, Hugh Doherty of Paris, J. S. Dwight, and W. H. Channing. The *New Times* further includes regular London and Paris correspondents, and, in imitation of the *Harbinger,* translations from 'solid and light literature of foreign languages' [57]— all of which, to the extent of sixty-four octavo pages to a number, appears to promise good value for the annual subscription of three dollars.

Channing noted the imminent advent of the *New Times* in his *Spirit of the Age,* tempering his welcome with the warning that James and Godwin carry Fourier's doctrine of Passional Attraction to pantheistic lengths. [58] He had, indeed, not long before, had occasion in reviewing James' *Moralism and Christianity* to open the eyes of the unwary to certain dangerous tendencies in that prophet's thought.[59] 'These lectures teach EGO–PANTHEISM,' he says, 'or that system of philosophy which regards every man as an incarnation of God; and they tend practically to produce that *lawless self-indulgence,* which, in all lands and ages has been the fruits of Idolatry."

The *New Times* never preached this seductive gospel, for it never preached at all; and we are left to conjecture whether the subscribers insufficiently subscribed or the editor lost interest in his project.[60]

VII

The lecture course reached the height of its popularity concurrently with the grand climacteric of the gospel according to Fourier. Mr James found employment along with the other spokesmen of social reform. The *Harbinger* advertises one course of 'lectures on Association' to be held at the N. Y. Medical College, the lecturers to comprise Horace Greeley, Ripley, Godwin, Macdaniel, Dana, and James.[61]

James lectured in Boston as well. His 'Socialism and Civilization' was delivered, at Emerson's invitation, before the Town and Country Club of that city, and there were doubtless other appearances. Emerson wrote of him (Nov. 1851), 'His lectures are really brilliant, and I was told that he swallowed up all the doctrinaires and neologists in New York, and is left sole aesthetic Doctor, *Doctor Dubitantium,* in that city'—to which he adds, 'He is the best man and companion in the world.' [62]

The lectures, which were read from manuscript, came subsequently to publication, at the author's own expense.[63] *What Constitutes the State* (1846) was followed by *Moralism and Christianity,* comprising two lectures read in New York and a third read in Boston. *Lectures and Miscellanies* printed at augmented length some discourses delivered in New York in the winter of 1850-1.

'Socialism and Civilization' best expresses James' attitude toward Associationism at this time. It pleads for no single panacea, urges the claims of no single Utopian theorist. 'By Socialism,' defines James, 'I mean not any special system of social organization, like that of Fourier, Owen, or St. Simon, but what is common to all these systems, namely, the idea of a perfect fellowship or society among men.' All these reformers differ, it is true, in matters of detail, but they agree in fundamentals: 'in holding our present social condition to be not only vicious, which everyone will admit, but also stupid, which is not so universally obvious. They declare that it is entirely competent to us at any time to organize relations of profound and enduring harmony among men, and thus to banish crime, vice, and suffering from the earth; and that nothing but an ignorance of the true principle of human nature stands between us and this most desirable consummation.'

Civilization, the present order of things in church

and state, holds the doctrine of man's natural depravity, supposing laws civil and ecclesiastical in consequence perpetually necessary to keeping the insubordi-
nate in check. Socialism, on the contrary, 'affirms the
inherent righteousness ["natural goodness"] of humanity, affirms that man is sufficient unto himself, and
needs no outward ordinances for his guidance, save
during his minority.' [64]

We are to judge between the claims upon us of
Socialism and Civilization by asking which furthers
man's destiny and highest life. What that destiny is,
Mr James has already told us: that spontaneous abandonment to our instincts and talents which avouches
the life of God in us. It is precisely this life which
finds little expression under 'civilization.' Concerned
with the physical and the moral, civilization 'affords
no succor to the divine [or aesthetic] life in man. Any
culture we can give to that life, is owing not to society,
but to our fortunate independence of it [such independence as James himself enjoyed]. For the inces-
sant action of society is to shut up all my time and
thought to the interests of my mere visible existence,
to the necessity of providing subsistence, education,
and social respect for myself and my children. To
these narrow limits society confines all my passion, all
my intellect, all my activity; and so far denies me self-
development.' [65]

Even what passes for Art, that which should proph-
esy the emancipation of all men from their servi-
tudes, now prostitutes itself all too frequently to the

basest of sycophancy. Society has 'no other conception of Art than as polished labor, labor stripped of its jacket and apron, and put into parlor costume. The Artist is merely the aboriginal ditcher refined into the painter, poet, or sculptor. Art [to society] is not the gush of God's life into every form of spontaneous speech and act; it is the talent of successfully imitating nature—the trick of a good eye, a good ear, or a good hand. . . .' Society tolerates the artist only on condition that he 'hallow, by every work of his hand, its existing prejudices and traditions; that he devote his perfectly docile genius to the consecration of its morality. If he would be truly its child, let him confine himself to the safe paths of portraiture and bust making, to the reproduction of the reigning sanctities in Church and State, their exemplary consorts and interesting families.' [66]

The evils of Civilization are patent. What does Socialism offer in its place? The whole promise of Socialism, replies Mr James, may thus be summarized: 'It promises to lift man out of the harassing bondage which he is under to nature and society, out of that crushing responsibility which he is under to both his own body and his fellow-man, and so leave him subject forever to God's unimpeded inspiration, leave him, in fact, the very play-thing of God, a mere pipe for the finger of Deity to play what stops it pleases. It proceeds upon a double postulate, namely, that every creature of God, by virtue of his creation, is entitled, 1, to an ample physical subsistence, that is, to the sat-

isfaction of all his natural appetites; 2, to an ample
social subsistence, that is, to the respect and affection
of every other creature of God.' [67]

In consequence of these postulates, Socialism 'con-
demns, after a certain stage of human progress, the
institution of limited property. . . . It aims indeed to
destroy all merely limited and conventional property,
all such property as is held not by any inward fitness
of the subject, but merely by external police or convention. . . .' After all, the institution of property
is no more a blessing to the property-holder than to
the propertyless. 'Nature and society should have no
power to identify me with a particular potato-patch
and in a particular family of mankind all my days.
The fact of my divine genesis makes God's whole
earth my home, makes all His children my intimates
and brethren . . . [Nature and society] but cheat me
when they give me houses and lands, and a score of
friends, and call these things my property. They
are not my property. My true property in nature includes all her strengths and sweetnesses, includes all
her resources to make pliant and strong and beautiful my body, and give my spirits the play of the
morning breeze. And my true property in mankind is not my mere natural father and mother and
brother and sister, and the great tiresome dispensation of uncles and aunts and cousins and nieces there-
unto appended, but the whole vast sweep of God's
harmonies in the realms of human passion, intellect
and action.' [68]

VIII

This was not, however, Mr James' final attitude towards socialism. Five years after the publication of 'Socialism and Civilization,' he had occasion, in one of his Letters to the *Tribune*,[69] to express himself on the relation of religion to economics and social systems; and he introduces Fourier and Comte to express his dissent from their naturalistic optimism. Society the natural state of man? How sanguine the view. Rather, society is the ultimate state, the Redeemed Form of Man, the Creator at last perfectly incarnated in the race.

'I distinctly aver that the proper earthly issue of Christianity is—I was very near saying Socialism. But Socialism means the doctrine of Fourier, or St. Simon, or Comte—means some special theory or other in regard to the organization of society.' Socialists proper all exhibit a mistaken theory of society. 'They all suppose it to be a product of purely natural laws.' But the world has yet to be convinced that 'Society' is possible. 'Fourier, for example, talks of organizing society as glibly as you would talk of organizing a military company. *But where is the society which is to be organized?* The very possibility of human society yet remains to be demonstrated.'[70]

Socialists hold that human nature is naturally good, and that the evils of the world have been caused by nothing more than inaccurate organization. Society, according to them, belongs to the realm of Nature, and requires, for its ultimating, merely the proper sort of manipulation. Christianity, on the contrary, holds to the doctrine of the Fall, and consequently regards Society as not the natural but the 'Redeemed Form of Man.' Human nature, human fellowship, human equality—James looks upon these 'not as a normal phenomenon of human nature, but only as the inseparable fruit of the travail of Christ's soul.'

Neither Fourier nor Comte 'assigns any scientific worth to Revelation'—which is to say, in James' terminology, that neither accepts the Christian view of man's native perversity and subsequent redemption. Fourier makes the social instinct 'date exclusively from the [natural] constitution of human nature, and this in spite of the ages of infernal discord and inequality between man and man, which all history avouches. [Yet] Surely, if human fellowship had been an outgrowth of human nature, we should have seen before this time some irrepressible exhibitions of it.' Actually, every practitioner of the Golden Rule will testify to having acted 'without any help from his nature, that is to say by the inspiration of a distinctly supernatural motive.' [71]

Comte 'takes no deeper view of the origin of society than the ordinary Socialist'; he supposes human society to be 'a purely physical phenomenon, or to be subject exclusively to natural laws.' And if he saw, clearly enough, the passing of existing theologies and philosophies, he confounded confusion by setting up his brand-new positivistic religion, 'with creed and catechism, fast and festival, duly appointed and established; and not merely a brand-new religion either, but a brand-new Deity also—a Deity so preposterous that only the rigidly "scientific intellect" which begot him could fail to be ashamed of him, for he is compounded of the abstract and metaphysical unity of all God's creatures, being in fact the aggregated scum or feculence of the universal finite experience.'[72]

IX

Thereafter we hear little of Fourier and his fellow Utopians.[73] William James tells us that Fourier's system was never displaced from his father's mind as 'at least a provisional representation of possible redeemed life,' but that 'at the last he cared little to dispute about matters of detail, being willing to cast the whole burden upon God, who would be sure to order it rightly when all the conditions were fulfilled.'[74]

It would be almost as true to say that James never concerned himself over the details of Fourier's system. If one reads Fourier or his expositors, one finds an abundance of pseudo-scientific exactness, a profusion of specific observations and prescriptions. The law is laid down with the minuteness of a Deuteronomy. With all this detail James never bothered, content merely to apprehend principles and make his own application of them. In a word, he read Fourier as he read Swedenborg, in a large-minded way, not as disciple or pedant.

A socialistic way of thinking remained with him to the end, but it remained 'a mere postulate or programme . . . and never received at his hands any concrete filling out.'[75]

Sporadic attempts at practical reform interested him little more than the details of social theory.

His opponent, Stephen Pearl Andrews, a man by no means lacking in astuteness, charged that James was 'of the class of purely ideal reformers, men who will lounge at their ease upon damask sofas and dream of a harmonic and beautiful world to be created hereafter, while they would probably be the very last to whom the earnest worker, in any branch of human concerns, could resort for aid with any prospect of success. He hates actual reform and reformers, and regards benevolence as a disease.' He is 'an astute and terribly searching and merciless . . . critic of the old, . . . who as respects the future, belongs to the school of seers and prophets, . . . a mere *jet d'eau* of aspiration, reaching a higher elevation at some point than any other man, but breaking into spray and impalpable mist, glittering in the sun, and descending to earth with no weight or mechanical force to effect any great end.'[76]

Much the same indictment must doubtless have been brought against Emerson, who equally dissociated himself from practical experiments like Brook Farm and the other phalanxes.

What deterred them? Not timidity or selfishness, surely. A sense of humor, rather; a detestation of earnest priggery; a suspicion of panaceas; a distrust of the sporadic; a judgment that little good is to be accomplished by establishing in some corner or other a community of superior, high-minded persons. Socialism is a mere toy when practised by a group: Fourier saw quite clearly that it could not possibly succeed unless the scale was grandiose. But for that scale, intellectual and emotional preparation is necessary. Socialism is primarily a spirit and only secondarily a method and system; and not the slightest good can come from reversing the order. Education, not Revolution.

In a very literal sense, James was a Fabian; and in the course of his long life he neither surrendered his conviction that the Day was just about to dawn, nor ever felt that it had.

Against all gainsaying, he held to his belief in 'the imminence of a transformation-scene in human affairs —"spiritually" speaking of course always—which was to be enacted somehow without gross or vulgar visibility, or at least violence, . . . but was none the less straining to the front, and all by reason of the world's being, deep within and at heart, as he conceived, so achingly anxious for it. He had the happiness—though not so untroubled, all the while, doubtless, as some of his declarations would appear to represent—of being able to see his own period and environment as the field of the sensible change, and thereby as a great historic hour. . . .' Yet when he was 'treated to any one of the loud vaticinations or particular revolutionary mes-

sages and promises our age was to have so much
abounded in, all his sense of proportion and of the
whole, of the real and the ridiculous, asserted itself
with the last emphasis.' [77]

A John the Baptist was this philosopher, a John the
Baptist with a sense of humor. The prophecy is none
the less earnest and insistent for the jocular idiom in
which it becomes articulate. The Day of the Lord
is at hand. Of day and hour, no man knows. But the
injunction persists: Watch.

CHAPTER VI

WILLIAM AND HENRY

I

The children were all born within six years: William in 1842; Henry in '43; Wilkinson in '45; Robertson in '46; and Alice in '48.

The care of a family so numerous, so various, so gifted would have made exacting demands upon any parent; and it was a matter of the greatest good fortune for the children, the two eldest in particular, that their father pursued no more exacting or sharply defined profession than that of 'philosopher,' and was in consequence as able as he was zealously willing to devote his fine intelligence to their education.

Tuition the boys had in abundance; but it was scattered and haphazard. Free, by its head's independence of shop and office, to live wherever living seemed at the moment most rich, the family moved restlessly about. If there was a consistency observable in the educational practise of the father, it was suspicion of all consistency, of all system, of all which hardens the individual into the type. Regular tuition, persistent drill, close specialization: these produce the scientist, the expert at research. But how shall they produce the versatile man, the artist, the philosopher? His sons were to covet the best gifts; to be *whole men,* not professionals. Detached from trade and from party, from the bigotries of patriotism and religion, they were to cultivate nothing less ample than the universally human.

Their whole manner of life set the family apart from others. The sons early felt, at first with bewilderment, the curious detachment of their parents from the interests of standard Americans.

Business, for example. In the America of Henry and William James' youth, not to have been immediately launched in business of a rigorous sort was to be suspect—'in the absence I mean of some fairly abnormal predisposition to virtue; since it was a world so simply constituted that whatever wasn't business, or exactly an office of a "store," places in which people sat close and made money, was just simply pleasure, sought, and sought only, in places in which people got tipsy.'[1]

The boys 'felt it tasteless and even humiliating that the head of our little family was *not* in business, and that even among our relatives on each side we couldn't so much as name proudly any one who was—with the sole exception of our maternal uncle Robertson Walsh, who looked, ever so benevolently, after our

father's "affairs" . . .' Their play-fellows spoke of their
father's business or profession; 'and I perfectly well
recover,' writes Henry, 'the effect of my own repeated
appeal to our parent for some presentable account of
him that would prove us respectable.'

The appeal only amused the father immensely. He
'put us off with strange unheard of attributions, such
as would have made us ridiculous in our special circles;
his "Say I'm a philosopher, say I'm a seeker for truth,
say I'm a lover of my kind, say I'm an author of books
if you like; or, best of all, just say I'm a Student" '—all
of which was of not the slightest help to boys. Robertson at last bravely answered the neighbors' interroga-
tives with the declaration that his father 'wrote,' and
that the visible fruit of his writing was *Lectures and
Miscellanies James.'* [2]

II

And then there was that other inevitable question:
'What church do *you* go to?' Another embarrassment:
The family was pewless.

For professional religion, their father felt sure, is
'the devil's masterpiece for ensnaring silly, selfish men.'
And this holds true for all its principal varieties:
'High Church,' Evangelical orthodoxy, and advanced
liberalism. There is 'Ritualism, intended to devour a
finer and fastidious style of men, men of sentiment and
decorum, cherishing scrupulously moderate views of
the difference between man and God'; and there is
'Revivalism, with a great red mouth intended to gobble

up a coarser sort of men, men for the most part of a fierce carnalism, of ungovernable appetite and passion, susceptible at best only of the most selfish hopes and the most selfish fears, toward God.' And then Bostonians have also to boast of 'a little indigenous bantam-cock which calls itself Radicalism, and which struts and crows, and scratches gravel in a manner so bumptious and peremptory, that I defy any ordinary barnyard chanticleer to imitate it.'ᵃ

Nothing, it appeared to him, could be 'more utterly worthless and even degrading, in a spiritual estimation, both to one's self and to society, than a life passed in ritual devotion, or the exercises of formal piety. It is an insult to God and man to dignify so sodden a routine with the sacred name of life; call it rather death and damnation to every soul of man *that finds it life.* . . . The visible Church seems to me in a spiritual or philosophic point of view to be "the abomination of desolation"; a refuge and embodiment of the frankest spiritual egotism and the rankest spiritual cupidity.'⁴

There was, accordingly, no family church, no family pew. But that a prohibition upon churchgoing would have lent it illegitimate attractions, James was of course shrewd enough to see. The children might visit any and all of the temples they fancied, and they did, at least during their childhood in New York. We 'sampled, in modern phrase, as small unprejudiced inquirers obeying their inspiration, any resort of any congregation detected by us; doing so, I make out moreover, with a sense of earnest provision for any contemporary challenge. "What church do you go to?" —the challenge took in childish circles that searching form; . . . To which I must add as well that our "fending" in this fashion for ourselves didn't so prepare us for invidious remark—remark I mean upon our pewless state, which involved, to my imagination, much the same discredit that a houseless or a cookless would have done—as to hush in my breast the appeal to our parents, not for religious instruction (of which we had plenty, and of the most charming and familiar) but simply for instruction (a very different thing) as to where we should say we "went," in our world, under cold scrutiny or derisive comment. It was colder than any criticism, I recall, to hear our father reply that we could plead nothing less than the whole privilege of Christendom, and that there was no communion, even that of the Catholics, even that of the Jews, even that of the Swedenborgians, from which we need find ourselves excluded.' [5]

This sweeping gesture did not much help the boys. For what was most of all embarrassing was just 'this particular crookedness of our being so extremely religious without having, as it were, anything in the least classified or striking to show for it. . . .'

In later life the younger Henry James professed to remember no clergymen who visited his father's house: 'They yet remaining for us, or at any rate myself, such

creatures of pure hearsay that when late in my teens
. . . I began to see them portrayed by George Eliot
and Anthony Trollope the effect was a disclosure of
a new and romantic species.' There was no technical
observance of Sunday, and whist was allowable then
as well as on week-days.

Spiritual and natural were not formally distinguished; secular and sacred blended into one within
the confines of the James home. The 'spiritual world'
lost its customary ominousness: 'We were in the habit
of hearing [it] as freely alluded to as we heard the
prospect of dinner or the call of the postman.'

The father's religion, Henry testifies, was 'more
deeply one with his life than I can conceive another
or a different case of its being,' for it was 'unaccom-
panied with a single one of the outward or formal,
the theological, devotional, ritual, or even implicitly
pietistic signs by which we usually know it.'[6]

Of course formal religious instruction quite lay outside James' scope or scheme. He liked indeed to read
the Bible to the boys in their younger days; but 'that
was the sole approach to a challenge of our complete
freedom of inward, not less than our natural ingenuity
of outward, experience. No other explicit address to
us in the name of the Divine could, I see, have been
made with any congruity—in the face of the fact that
invitations issued in all the vividest social terms, terms
of living appreciation, of spiritual perception, of "human fellowship," to use the expression that was perhaps oftenest on his lips and his pen alike, were the

very substance of the food supplied in the parental nest.'[7]

And explicit *moral* instruction was quite as much wanting as religious. What point in sedulously guarding the children from that species of Pharisaic pride which distinguishes the *elect,* if they were only to fall prey to the worse plague of *moralism?*

For all the boys' bewilderment at the uniqueness of their situation, they came—even Henry, whose turn of mind differed most from the father's—to understand what sort of conviction underlay his whimsical denunciations of virtue and piety. His prime horror was of *prigs;* 'he cared only for virtue that was more or less ashamed of itself. . . . The presence of paradox was so bright among us—though fluttering ever with as light a wing and as short a flight as need have been —that we fairly grew used to allow, from an early time, for the so many and odd declarations we heard launched, to the extent of happily "discounting" them; the moral of all of which was that we need never fear to be good enough if we were only social enough: a splendid meaning indeed being attached to the latter term. Thus we had ever the amusement, since I can really call it nothing less, of hearing morality, or moralism, as it was more invidiously worded, made hay of in the very interest of character and conduct; these things suffering much, it seemed, by their very association with the conscience—that is the *conscious* conscience—the very home of the literal, the haunt of so many pedantries.'[8]

III

The barest chronicle of the sons' schooling attests the thoroughness with which their detachment was pursued.

'We were day-boys, William and I,' the younger Henry writes, 'at dispensaries of learning, the number and succession of which today excite my wonder; we couldn't have changed oftener . . . if our presence had been inveterately objected to, and yet I enjoy an inward certainty that, my brother being vividly bright and I quite blankly innocuous, this reproach was never brought home to our house.'

There was first a series of governesses, ending with French and Russian recruits. Then came a series of boys' schools: the Institution Vergnes, on lower Broadway; the quieter haven of Mr Richard Pulling Jenks' institution; the establishment of Forest and Quackenbush, one of long and excellent standing, where two or three of the boys' New York uncles had been formed.[9]

But already in 1849, James was writing Emerson: 'considering with mock pity our four stout boys, who have no play-room within doors and import shocking bad manners from the street, we gravely ponder whether it wouldn't be better to go abroad for a few years with them, allowing them to absorb French and German and get such a sensuous education as they can't get here.'[10]

At last in 1855, the family were conveyed across the

ocean in the steamer "Atlantic"; and the boys added to
their American miscellany a stock of European tuition quite as varied and casual. The Pensionat Roediger,
at Geneva, for the first season: mild, genial, humane;
conspicuous for its amenity betwixt master and pupil.
There had been some preliminary tasting of the more
celebrated Institution Haccius, the customary resort of
young Americans; but there, the American language
reigned supreme, while at the Roediger, 'the English
jostled the American, the Russian the German, and
there even trickled through a little funny French.' [11]

But though they had fared across the sea 'under
the glamour of the Swiss school in the abstract,' the
parental impatience at the regular and ordered soon
broke out; and, stopping briefly at Paris *en route,* they
moved to London for the winter, locating first in
Berkeley Street and afterward in St. John's Wood, near
their friends, the Wilkinsons.

The parents would have none of the day school near
home, and as for the 'public school,' the boarding
school, that 'they saw as a fearful and wonderful,
though seemingly effective, preparation of the young
for English life and an English career, but related to
that situation only. . . . They had doubtless heard
claimed for it just that no other method for boys *was*
so splendidly general, but they had,' writes Henry,
'their own sense of the matter. . . .' Which is to say
that the English gentleman, of correct public school
and university training, admirable as he must be confessed, yet failed to satisfy the Jameses. [12]

They settled down to the services of a Scotch tutor.
Transported to Paris, they first took on a French tutor,
a pallid-faced minor poet, whose instructions filled in
the intervals between walks along the quays and visits
to the Louvre.[13]

There followed another 'school'—of a sort: the Institution Fezandie in Rue Balzac, 'a social, rather than
tuitional house.' M. Fezandie was 'an active and sympathetic ex-Fourierist' ('I think,' adds Henry, 'there
were only ex-Fourierists by that time'); doubtless Mr
James had heard of him as still cherishing the by now
lost hope. The Institution had embarked on an experiment, 'if not absolutely phalansteric at least inspired, or at any rate enriched, by a bold idealism. I
like,' Henry continues, 'to think of the Institution as
all but phalansteric—it so corrects any fear that such
places might be dreary. I recall this one as positively
gay—bristling and bustling and resonant. . . .' The
'phalansteric' character of the whole consisted in its
range of pensioner-students, extending, male and fe-
male, from infancy to senectude, though principally
Anglo-Saxons. 'I recover it as for ourselves a beautifully
mixed adventure, a brave little seeing of the world on
the happy pretext of "lessons." We *had* lessons from
time to time, but had them "in company with ladies
and gentlemen. . . ."' Here French was the language
of the family; and the youngest Anglo-Saxons ('we
three' in particular) fared better as to fluency than the
older virgins and youths.[14]

That episode, too, came to an end; 'the general enterprise simply proved a fantasy not workable.' The boys were transported to Boulogne-sur-Mer, there to attend the *Collège* through the winter of 1857-8. William experienced there his first experience of thorough teaching, gained his first conception of earnest work. Henry had less of the *Collège* than William and Wilky; after a few weeks an illness drew him away, and for the rest of the winter he sat privately under the tuition of 'that decayed classicist,' M. Ansiot.[15]

A return to America for a year, with Newport as focus; then another European migration—to Geneva, for the winter of 1859-60. Here William entered the Academy (subsequently aggrandized into University). Henry was first placed at another Institution, the *École Préparatoire aux Écoles Spéciales* of M. Rochette, scientific in curriculum. A curious choice on the parents' part, for Henry ever found himself helpless in the presence of the most trifling addition or subtraction. Perhaps it represented, contrary to the usual 'liking for us after a gasp or two whatever we seemed to like,' a momentary instinct on the parents' part toward the principle of discipline or at any rate balance: a sense that Henry's *literary* vent needed curbing in the interests of some more generally extended and developed personality.[16]

Relenting came speedily, at all events; and presently 'literature' formed the sole fare. There were private readings with tutors: French with one; Virgil and Livy with another; Schiller and Lessing with a third. The Academy was open as well: 'My dear parents, as if to make up to me, characteristically, for my recent absurd strain to no purpose [at the Institution Rochette], allowed me now the happiest freedom, left me to attend such lectures as I preferred, only desiring that I should attend several a week, and content . . . that these should involve neither examinations nor reports.'[17]

For the summer of 1860 the boys were packed off to Bonn-am-Rhein, where, under the care of a couple of friendly pedagogues, they were to pick up German, a language and a consciousness—whatever was 'characteristically German, and therein freshly vivid—with the great vividness that, by our parents' vague wish, we were all three after or out for. . . .'[18]

IV

Two tastes William early exhibited. At fifteen, his joy over a microscope, Christmas gift from his father, knew no bounds, and at Geneva he began to study anatomy, quite by himself. Then before he had reached his teens, he was constantly and copiously drawing—'easily, freely, and, as who should say, infallibly . . .' In Paris he had better instruction in drawing than before; and from Bonn he wrote a Genevan associate, 'Je me suis pleinement décidé à éssayer le métier de peintre.'

Full consent to this decision was at first withheld. Mr James offered 'the rarest in all the so copious annals

of parental opposition to the aesthetic as distinguished
from some other more respectable course.' Americans
enough, Anglo-Saxons enough, found 'art' impractica-
ble, commercially unsuccessful, disreputable. Mr
James objected on none of these grounds. 'What was
marked in our father's prime uneasiness in presence
of any particular form of success we might, according
to our lights as then glimmering, propose to invoke
was that it bravely, or with such inward assurance,
dispensed with any suggestion of an alternative. What
we were to do instead was just to *be* something, something unconnected with specific doing, something free
and uncommitted, something finer in short than being
that, whatever it was, might consist of.'

The return of the Jameses to Newport was understood to be motivated by this decision of William's:
'Since William was to embrace the artistic career—and
freedom for this experiment had been after all, as I repeat that it was always in like cases to be, not in the least
grudgingly granted him—our return to America would
place him in prompt and happy relation to William
Hunt, then the most distinguished of our painters as
well as one of the most original and delightful of
men. . . .'

Puzzling that, at the mid-century, one should *leave*
Europe in order to take up the serious study of painting! Henry admits that 'never surely had so odd a
motive operated for a break with the spell of Paris.'
Yet this was, indeed, at the time 'judged among us
at large, other considerations aiding, a sound basis for

action,' and was the motive generally and sincerely enough named.[19]

V

The family settled at Newport, with its opera-glass turned forever across the sea, Newport, 'comparatively, and in its degree incurably, cosmopolite. . . .'

By its character of watering-place, Newport offered a refuge to those who followed no 'business'; as Henry puts it, 'imposed itself at that period to so remarkable a degree as the one right residence, in all our great country, for those tainted, under whatever attentuations, with the quality and effect of detachment.'[20]

For a year, William worked daily in the studio of William Hunt, along with John LaFarge, to whose elegant dominance of the scene Henry has paid tribute in *Notes*. Henry nominally studied English and Latin literature with the curate of Trinity Church; but he spent stray and happy hours in Hunt's studio copying casts. These were what counted: They hovered about 'Art.' Hunt, and still more LaFarge, was all artist.[21]

Two contemporaries of William and Henry, T. S. Perry and E. W. Emerson, have left vivid sketches of the James family during its sojourn in Newport.

Perry was Henry's special friend, and the boys went for long walks in the afternoon. They discussed Fourier. 'Harry had heard his father describe the great reformer's proposal to establish universal happiness, and like a good son he tried to carry the good news further.' Henry fell under the influence of Ruskin, and painstakingly copied leaves and rocks as well as casts, but his chief interest already lay in literature: the *Revue des Deux Mondes* was Henry's special stay, his solace for the want of Europe. He wrote stories in imitation of his favorite Balzac; he translated De Musset's *Lorenzaccio.*

Perry was struck with the combination, in James family's relation to one another, of merciless criticism and satire with the most loyal affection. The father set the tone; and unlike some humorists he took a joke as amiably as he made one. When he was about to bring out his *Substance and Shadow,* William amused the family 'by designing a small cut to be put on the title page, representing a man beating a dead horse. This will illustrate the joyous chaff that filled the Jameses' house. There was no limit to it. There were always books to tell about and laugh over, or to admire, and there was an abundance of good talk with no shadow of pedantry or priggishness.' [22]

Mealtimes were always exciting. Emerson's son Edward, who spent the spring vacations of 1860 and '61 at Newport with the Jameses, describes a specimen. ' "The adipose and affectionate Wilky," as his father called him, would say something and be instantly corrected or disputed by the little cock-sparrow Bob, the youngest, but good-naturedly defend his statement, and then Henry would emerge from his silence in defence of Wilky. ["Henry's spirits were never so high as the others. If they had been, he still would have

had but little chance in a conflict of wits with them, on
account of his slow speech, his halting choice of words
and phrases. . . ."] Then Bob would be more imperti-
nently insistent, and Mr James would advance as
Moderator, and William, the eldest, join in. The voice
of the Moderator presently would be drowned by the
combatants and he soon came down vigorously into
the arena, and when, in the excited argument, the
dinner-knives might not be absent from eagerly ges-
ticulating hands, dear Mrs James, more conventional,
but bright as well as motherly, would look at me, laugh-
ingly reassuring, saying, "Don't be disturbed; they
won't stab each other. This is usual when the boys
come home [Wilky and Bob were fellow-students of
Edward Emerson's at Mr F. B. Sanborn's school in
Concord]" . . . Mr James considered this debate,
within bounds, excellent for the boys. In their speech
singularly mature and picturesque, as well as vehement,
the Gaelic element in their descent always showed.
Even if they blundered, they saved themselves by
wit.' [28]

VI

And now there came a sudden change in William's
plans—his interest in the practise of painting suddenly
ceased; 'a turn of our affair attended, however, with
no shade of commotion, no repining at proved waste;
with as little of any confessed ruefulness of mistake on
one side as of any elation of wisdom, any resonance
of the ready "I told you so" on the other,' the father's.

This was quite in character. So repellant did Mr James find the more palpable and vulgar sorts of success, as well as the more arrogant varieties of godliness, that a false start was, to him, at least as rich and significant as an unerring accuracy of aim. 'I am not sure indeed,' writes Henry, apropos of this very incident, 'that the kind of personal history most appealing to my father would not have been some kind that should fairly proceed by mistakes, mistakes more human, more associational [an echo of Fourierism], less angular, less hard for others, that is less exemplary for them (since righteousness, as mostly understood, was in our parent's view, I think, the cruellest thing in the world) than straight and smug and declared felicities.' [24]

In Mr James' later books, the problem of *waste* ever turns up; the triumphant conversion of waste—*hell, that is*—into fruitful land. It constituted a principal interest of his in daily life as well as speculation: How to convert, transform, transmute. The younger Henry writes: 'I find myself thinking of our life in those years as profiting greatly for animation and curiosity by the interest he shed for us on the whole side of the human scene usually held least interesting—the element, the appearance, of *waste,* which plays there such a part and into which he could read under provocation so much character and colour and charm, so many implications of the fine and the worthy, that, since, the art of missing or of failing, or of otherwise going astray, did after all in his hands escape becom-

ing either a matter of real example or of absolute pre-
cept, enlarged not a little our field and our categories
of appreciation and perception. . . . Which means, to
my memory, that we breathed somehow an air in which
waste, for us at least, couldn't and didn't live, so certain were aberrations and discussions, adventures, ex-
cursions and alarms of whatever sort, to wind up in
a "transformation scene" . . . ; a figuration of each
involved issue and item before the footlights of a
familiar idealism, the most socialised and ironised,
the most amusedly generalised, that possibly could
be.'[25]

If not a painter's training, why not a 'college education'? Why, indeed, should not both William and
Henry have been sent to 'college'? Their father was
a Union graduate; many of their friends were Harvard men. Yet James displayed 'extreme tepidity'
towards the notion of sending his sons. 'I make out in
him,' says Henry, 'and at the time made out, a great
revulsion of spirit from that incurred experience in his
own history, a revulsion I think moreover quite independent of any particular or intrinsic attributes of
the seat of learning involved in it.'

During a holiday spent at their grandmother's in
Albany, the sons journeyed to Schenectady, filled
with 'college spirit,' looking forward to the time when
they too should wear such 'society' badges and trinkets
as adorned the person of the undergraduate who acted
as cicerone. But nothing came of it; and the parents
appeared left equally cold by Brown, Columbia, Yale,

—all near at hand. 'Even Harvard, clearly—and it was perhaps a trifle odd—moved him in our interest as little as Schenectady could do. . . .' The father's imagination possessed 'no grain of susceptibility to what might have been, on the general ground, "socially expected." ' [26]

What, precisely, constituted Mr James' objection to a university education? In part, surely, his judgment that it offered a fare intellectually, and still more spiritually, sterile. James had no inclination to exalt 'book-learning'; he placed no extravagant valuation upon the classics; and, though Locke had been displaced from preëminence as staple in philosophical instruction, he was not likely to look upon Bishop Butler and Hamilton (the successors) as more profitable. Yet one who conjectured James' chief repugnance to be against the 'socially expected' and the socially discriminatory would be correct. At the Radical Club, he was heard to affirm that 'the rage for multiplying schools and colleges in our country was a real insanity, as promoting an exclusively personal or isolated culture among us, and to that extent retarding the development of a common or public consciousness.' The condition of England seemed to him proof of his contention, for there was a nation 'spiritually rotting from excessive personal culture, or the over-education of a scholarly class, which could do nothing but criticise, from its own idle, luxurious point of view, every scheme that looked to distinctively general or race culture. . . .' [27]

As between experience, as varied and rich as possible, of places and persons, and a diet of lectures, textbooks, and fraternities, the choice stood indubitably sure.

VII

'College' was skipped; and when the versatile William turned from art to science, he headed directly for illiberal specialization. In 1861 he registered for the study of chemistry at the Lawrence Scientific School of Harvard, working in the laboratory under Charles W. Eliot. In 1863 he transferred to the department of Anatomy; and the next year, to the Medical School.

For some puzzling reason, in 1862 Henry followed William to Cambridge, there to attend lectures at the Law School. Why deprecate the 'college course' so vehemently, 'only so soon afterwards to forswear all emphasis and practically smile, in mild oblivion, on *any* Harvard connection I might find it in me to take up . . .'?

Yet Henry was not disposed to refuse. For himself, the career of the imagination was the only conceivable one, and as for education in the conventional sense, he felt sincerely indifferent to whether he was exposed to it or not. He shrank from asking exemption on the ground that he meant to be an 'artist': such a begging-off struck him as presumptuous. The claim to be 'literary' could only be justified by one's performance: a bare-faced *claim* was barefaced indeed.

A 'physical mishap' terminated his days at the Law

School; and he took delighted refuge again in his reading.

In 1864 the rest of the James family moved to Boston, settling in Ashburton Place; subsequently, in 1866, they moved to Cambridge, there to end their career of wanderings. William accompanied Agassiz to the Amazon, studied medicine in Germany, began in 1873 his teaching at Harvard. Henry began his friendships with Norton and Howells, began to contribute stories and reviews to the *Atlantic* (of which Howells was then assistant editor) and the *Galaxy*.[28]

When Henry began to write, his father subjected the notion to the same criticism he had visited upon William's painting: 'it was breathed upon me with the finest bewildering eloquence, with a power of suggestion in truth which I fairly now count it a gain to have felt play over me, that this too was narrowing.'

Having heard objection fairly stated, Henry, like William, was at liberty to do as he chose; and his father's love and pride offered his career the most zealous support. Already in 1868 James is writing his friend Fields, then editor of the *Atlantic,* who had ventured to publish some remarks on Henry's writing: 'I had no sooner left your sanctum yesterday than I was afflicted to remember how I had profaned it by my unmeasured talk about poor H. Please forget it utterly. I don't know how it is with better men, but the parental sentiment is so fiendish a thing with me, that if anyone attempt to slay my young, especially in a clandestine way, or out of a pious regard (*e.g.*)

to the welfare of the souls comprised in the diocese of the Atlantic, I can't help devoting him bag and baggage to the infernal gods.' [29]

VIII

The results of this strange educational policy proved on the whole singularly happy. Henry was ever given the freedom his development required: to taste, to try, to travel, to observe. A shy and timid boy, he was offered, in his father and mother and William, love of the most full and sustaining sort along with the keenest play of criticism. William's more vigorous and aggressive if not so clearly defined nature might have battled its way through any sort of youthful disadvantage; but Henry's genius was in kind so precious that without Europe, and a civilized home and conversation, and access to the best society, English and American, he must have been *manqué* indeed.

What Henry drew from his tutelage was in short the sense that experience is not enough: it must be interpreted. The crude ore must be refined till the pure gold of significance shall emerge. Analysis, perception, apprehension. It seemed to him that his parents had, for the direction of their children's course, the one counsel, Convert, convert. 'With which I have not even the sense of any needed appeal in us for further apprehension of the particular precious metal our chemistry was to have in view. I taste again in that pure air no ghost of a hint, for instance, that the precious

metal was the refined gold of "success"—a reward of
effort for which I remember to have heard at home
no good word, nor any sort of word, even faintly
breathed. . . . We were to convert and convert, success—in the sense that was in the general air—or no
success; and simply everything that should happen
to us, every contact, every impression and every experience we should know, were to form our soluble
stuff, with only ourselves to thank should we remain
unaware, by the time our perceptions were decently
developed, of the substance finally projected and most
desirable.' [30]

The beauty of the understanding between Henry
James and his father lies in its triumph over divergent
temperaments, opposed methods of vision. Henry was
an artist; his father, a philosopher. Persons, and the
relations they sustained to one another, were Henry's
subjects; the father rejected persons in favor of the
universally human. Henry described and analyzed a
disappearing society; his father prophecied a Society
to come. Henry turned for his criterion to the aristo-
crat, subtle in his sense of values, whose conscience
had been transmuted into taste; his father, to the man
on the street, who possessed no self-conscious individ-
uality to interpose between his fellow and God. One
found his Shekinah in the drawing room; the other,
in the horse car.

How could Henry have heeded Swedenborg's dic-
tum that to think spiritually is not to think in terms
of persons; how could he have entered into his father's

eager search for the Creator behind his creatures, the
Absolute beyond the phenomenal? His whole temperament cried out for an opposite 'revelation.' Early,
he was conscious that, in contrariety to his father's
Secret, his 'small uneasy mind . . . attached its gaping
view . . . to things and persons, objects and aspects,
frivolities all, I dare say I was willing to grant, com-
pared with whatever manifestations of the serious,
these being by need, apparently, the abstract; and that
in fine I should have been thankful for a state of faith,
a conviction of the Divine, an interpretation of the
universe . . . which would have supplied more features or appearances.'

Henry felt quite clearly that he 'gaped imaginatively'
to a set of relations very different from those at which
his father gaped. 'I couldn't have framed stories that
would have succeeded in involving the least of the
relations that seemed most present to *him;* while those
most present to myself, that is more complementary
to whatever it was I thought of as humanly most interesting, attaching, inviting, were the ones his schemes
of importances seemed virtually to do without.' [81]

Yet for all this contrariety between the philosophical
temper and the literary, between that delight in the
broad and democratic and universal which was his
father's and that in the particular and subtle and
aristocratic, in the fine shades and subtle distinctions
between persons and relationships, which was his, he
could not but recognize his father as transcending his
profession and his creed: spontaneously abandoning

himself as much as ever any 'artist' to the person and the moment, the savor of the unique experience. For all his devotion to the *Maximus Homo,* James had as keen a palate for the infinite distinctions between one man and another; and his sense of humor knew no dulling at the hands of the abstract, which indeed but whetted his taste for the concrete. Never truly had the Absolute been embraced by so hearty a lover.

'If he so endeared himself,' Henry writes of his father, 'wasn't it . . . through his never having sentimentalised or merely meditated away, so to call it, the least embarrassment of the actual about him, and having with a passion peculiarly his own kept together his stream of thought, however transcendent and the stream of life, however humanised? There was a kind of experiential authority in his basis, as he felt his basis —there being no human predicament he couldn't by a sympathy more *like* direct experience than any I have known enter into . . .'

'Father's ideas' lay outside Henry's range, but his comprehension of his father's powers and spirit put out of the question the belief that they could be anything but true—or if not true, then something much deeper and better. 'Detached as I could during all those years perhaps queerly enough believe myself, it would still have done my young mind the very greatest violence to have to suppose that any plane of conclusion for him, however rich and harmonious he might tend to make conclusion, could be in the nature of a fool's paradise. . . . Small vague outsider as I was, I couldn't have borne *that* possibility; and I see, as I return to the case, how little I really could ever have feared it. No, I feel myself complacently look back to *my* never having, even at my small poorest, been so *bête,* either, as to conceive he might be "wrong," wrong as a thinker-out, in his own way, of the great mysteries, because of the interest and amusement and vividness his attesting spirit could fling over the immediate ground. . . . If it didn't sound in a manner patronising I should say that I saw that my father saw. . . .' [82]

The same spirit breathes in a letter he wrote William after the publication of their father's *Literary Remains:* 'How intensely original and personal his whole system was, and how indispensable it is that those who go in for religion should take some heed of it. I can't enter into it (much) myself—I can't be so theological. . . . But I can enjoy greatly the spirit, the feeling, and manner of the whole . . . , and feel really that poor Father, struggling so alone all his life, and so destitute of every worldly or literary ambition, was yet a great writer.' [33]

Attempts to connect the writing of the elder Henry James and the younger appear futile. It has been alleged, by a generally astute critic, that the 'same qualities are present in both . . . the same subtlety of thought, the same precision of language . . .' [34] These qualities the novelist indeed possessed, but neither the father nor William, both of whom were *rich* rather than *fine.*

The novelist's 'moral neutrality' or 'æsthetic morality,' as it has variously been termed, seems, indeed,
a kind of reflection of the elder Henry James' Beyond
Moralism. But the resemblance is superficial. The
ladies and gentlemen of the novelist's world escape
gross sinning partly by their thinness of blood, partly
by their breeding, partly by their aristocratic code of
niceness; but the 'artists' of the elder Henry James,
the 'men of destiny,' are to transcend the Decalogue
by the exuberance of their humanity.

IX

As for William James, he 'seldom referred to his
schooling with anything but contempt, and usually
dismissed all reference to it by saying that he "never
had any." ' In 1867 he wrote from Germany to his
friend, Tom Ward, lamenting his lack of *facts:* 'If
I had been *drilled* further in mathematics, physics,
chemistry, logic, and the history of metaphysics, and
had established, even if only in my memory, a firm
and thoroughly familiar *basis* of knowledge in all
these sciences . . . , instead of having now to keep
going back and picking up loose ends of these elements . . . , I might be steadily advancing.' [35] His
haphazard schooling could not of course assure the
sort of grounding he here confesses the lack of, and
was hardly the training for a pure scientist—or pure
logician either, for that matter.

But if his education unfitted him for any narrow

specialization, it was admirably adapted to foster the freshness and vivacity of response with which William James all his life greeted the new experience, the lack of conventional and professional inhibitions, the extraordinary richness and variety of his interests. On the negative, the fluidity of his early life freed him from falling into any conventionalized attitudes; on the positive, it meant 'quickening collision with places, people, and ideas at a rate at which such contacts are not vouchsafed to many schoolboys.' At nineteen he already had acquired the most spontaneous cosmopolitanism: followed the French and English reviews and books, paintings, public affairs, characterizing people and peoples with acumen and literary skill.

William's son and biographer remarks truly upon the easy assurance with which, in his maturity, William James passed from one field of inquiry to another—all in a fashion quite unconsciously audacious; and he quite justly credits the circumstances of William's youth with having 'fostered and corroborated this native mobility and detachment of mind.'[36]

William was assuredly his father's special joy and pride. He 'apprehended ever so deeply and tenderly his eldest son's . . . genius—as to which he was to be so justified'; though when the son abandoned art for science, taking up in succession chemistry, anatomy, physiology, medicine, psychology, philosophy, 'the rich *malaise* at every turn characteristically betrayed itself, each of these surrenders being, by the measure of them

in the parental imagination, so comparatively narrowing.' [37]

In his intellectual progress William drew steadily
closer to his father.

During his earlier studies in science, he was a thorough-going naturalist, sceptical of idealism, especially
the intuitive sort; at the age of twenty-five he wrote
his father, from Germany, an incisive statement of
their differences:

'I have read your article [38] . . . several times care-
fully. I must confess that the darkness which to me
has always hung over what you have written on these
subjects is hardly at all cleared up. Every sentence
seems written from a point of view which I nowhere
get within range of, and on the other hand ignores
all sorts of questions which are visible from my present view. My questions, I know, belong to the Understanding, and I suppose deal entirely with the "natural
constitution" of things; but I find it impossible to
step out from them into relation with "spiritual" facts.
. . . I feel myself in fact more and more drifting
towards the sensationalism closed in by scepticism—
but the scepticism will keep bursting out in the very
midst of it, too, from time to time; so that I cannot
help thinking I may one day get a glimpse of things
through the ontological window. At present it is
walled up. I can understand now no more than ever
the world-wide gulf you put between "Head" and
"Heart"; to me they are inextricably entangled together, and seem to grow from a common stem. . . .' [39]

To all of which his father rejoined, 'I am sure I have something better to tell you than you will be able to learn from all Germany—at least all scientific Germany.'[40]

But six years later, in 1873, William has already renounced his materialism, to the great joy of his father, who writes of him to Henry:

'He had a great effusion. I was afraid of interfering with it, or possibly checking it, but I ventured to ask what especially in his opinion had produced the change. He said several things: the reading of Renouvier (particularly his vindication of the freedom of the will) and of Wordsworth, whom he has been feeding on now for a good while; but more than anything else, his having given up the notion that all mental disorder requires to have a physical basis. This had become perfectly untrue to him. He saw that the mind does act irrespectively of material coercion, and could be dealt with therefore at first hand, and this was health to his bones. It was a splendid declaration, and though I had known from unerring signs of the fact of the change, I never had been more delighted than by hearing of it so unreservedly from his own lips. He has been shaking off his respect for men of mere science as such, and is even more universal and impartial in his mental judgments than I have known him before. . . .'[41]

In the last letter William ever wrote his father he suggested the making of 'a collection of *extracts* from your various writings . . . , after the manner of the extracts from Carlyle, Ruskin, and Co . . . I have long thought such a volume would be the best monument to you.' [42]

After the elder James' death this plan took modified expression in a volume of 'literary remains' upon the editing of which William spent the summer of 1884. He prefaced the whole with an admirably sympathetic exposition of his father's thought, supplemented on every theme by generous 'extracts' from his father's published works. The task of editing proved a happy one, for in its process William felt himself 'sinking into an intimacy' with his father to a degree which he had never before enjoyed. [43]

To any appreciation of his father's writings William always responded gratefully, especially when the appreciation was wrung from a professional philosopher like his friend Shadworth Hodgson.

In 1885 he wrote of his father to Hodgson: 'He was like Carlyle in being no *reasoner* at all, in the sense in which philosophers are reasoners. Reasoning was only an unfortunate necessity of exposition for them both. . . . As you say, the world of his thought had a few elements and no others ever troubled him. *Those* elements were very deep ones, and had theological names. . . . I wish that somebody could *take up* something from his system into a system more articulately scientific.' [44]

William James worked his way free of the implied criticism of his father's intuitive thought as he had worked his way free of materialism. By the time of

A Pluralistic Universe, he is asking, 'Who cares for Carlyle's reasons, or Schopenhauer's or Spencer's? A philosophy is the expression of a man's intimate character. . . . If we take the whole history of philosophy, the systems reduce themselves to a few main types which, under all the technical verbiage in which the ingenious intellect of man envelopes them, are just so many visions, modes of feeling the whole push, and seeing the whole drift of life, forced on one by one's total character and experience, and on the whole *preferred*. . . .'[45]

At the end of his life, William James could have written with yet greater conviction those moving lines he addressed to his dying father: 'All my intellectual life I owe to you; and though we have often seemed at odds in the expression thereof, I'm sure there's a harmony somewhere, and that our strivings will combine. What my debt to you is goes beyond all my power of estimating,—so early, so penetrating and so constant has been the influence.'[46]

X

Facile conjecture has attempted to find a paternity for William James' 'mysticism' and his 'pluralistic universe' in his Swedenborgian inheritance.[47] The conjectures require but summary treatment. The popular view that Swedenborgians are a dreamy and *mystical* people is ludicrously inaccurate: they are, for the most part, especially sane and sensible and practical.

And the elder James, whose Swedenborgianism was of course *sui generis,* can be called a mystic in no more precise sense than that he steadfastly credited his highest aspirations with telling him the substantial truth about the universe; that, confronted with occasional oppositions of head and heart, he steadfastly chose to regard the heart as the primary fount of knowledge. He practised no ascetic rigors, suffered no trances, laid claim to no special revelations. He denounced spiritism.

As for James' *pluralism,* it so little springs either from his father's reading or his own that already in the introduction to *Literary Remains* he intimates his own pluralistic sympathies in distinction to his father's monism. He contrasts the 'healthy-minded moralist' with the 'sick man,' the religionist, the twice-born. 'Any absolute moralism is a pluralism,' he points out; 'any absolute religion is a monism. It shows the depth of Mr James' religious insight that he first and last and always made moralism the target of his hottest attack, and pitted religion and it against each other as enemies. . . .'[48]

'Pragmatism' and the 'will to believe' might more fairly be charged to the account of the elder James, for the epistemological passages in his works breathe the same scorn of Hegel and German dialectic, the same emphasis on the *heart* and the *will,* as do his son's.[49] Much of the brilliant attack on intellectualism in the early chapters of *A Pluralistic Universe* might, in fact, have been indited by William's father.

The specific influence of Swedenborg on William James was as slight as his knowledge. His attitude toward his father's Seer was, throughout his life, one of respect and interest. He defended Swedenborg against the popular imputation of insanity: 'If you class Swedenborg as crazy, you will have to change the meaning of crazy.' He told one of his students, 'If I were limited to a single book, there is no book that I would prefer to Swedenborg.' [50] He is said to have cherished the intention of one day writing a book on Swedenborg.[51] But he was never limited to a single book, and the *day* never came. Find time to master the *Arcana* or even to study it seriously he never did.

Beyond gainsaying, however, the elder James' addiction to Swedenborg collaborated with William's own temperamental impatience of the merely technical and academic. William knew his father possessed of too keen a mind and too firm a hold on reality ever to be dismissed as crank or fanatic; and so striking an instance of mental vigor and sanity outside the academe must preclude hasty generalizations. The professional philosopher's sneer at Swedenborg and at the amateurs of philosophy in general (like the elder Henry James) was forbidden him. Like his father, he was willing to give respectful though by no means credulous or uncritical hearing to men who owned no dignity of professorial chair and had never mastered the history of metaphysics and could not use the technical vocabulary.

Sharing his father's philosophic as well as personal

democracy, William James was willing to study popular religion as well as theology. In 1891, he speaks of himself as 'turning for light in the direction of all sorts of despised spiritualistic and unscientific ideas. Father would find in me today a much more receptive listener—all *that* philosophy has got to be brought in.'[52]

The strongest resemblances between father and son were not doctrinal in any exact sense but temperamental: both were optimists, democrats, men of warm, large, generous natures. Their literary styles were extraordinarily alike: both wrote philosophy with verve and humor, with audacity of metaphor, with diction ranging from the learned to the racy. How true of the elder Henry James is Santayana's remark of William: 'While he shone in expression and would have wished his style to be noble if it could also be strong, he preferred in the end to be spontaneous, and to leave it at that: he tolerated slang in himself rather than primness.'[53] But indeed for most of the literary portraits of William James one encounters, the elder Henry James might quite as well have sat.[54]

CHAPTER VII

LAST YEARS

I

THE professed reason for the return to America had been William's adoption of the artistic career. But Henry felt, even at the time, that it was a reason so very curious as to invite one to conjecture another. Was there not a 'parental homesickness'? 'I am of course not sure how often our dear father may not explicatively have mentioned the shy fact that he himself in any case had gradually ceased to "like" Europe.'[1]

Confessed or unconfessed, the change of heart came naturally enough. The elder James scarcely lent himself to the rôle of avowed and permanent exile. He was a democrat both by temperament and by conviction; and the aristocratic cast of European society grew more and more to irritate him. Even England, with its pretensions to liberalism, did not satisfy. In fact, just as Anglican claims irritated him more rather than less than Roman claims—as being more presumptuous and more absurd in a body which accorded liberty to conflicting voices, so constitutional monarchy and the actual sovereignty of Parliament merely aggravated, to his mind, the crying shame of social gradations.

During his stay in Europe, James contributed to the New York *Tribune* a series of letters, running to fourteen,[2] which is said to have attracted much attention—why it is a little difficult to see, for James had scant interest in the picturesque detail and scant taste for gossip: the letters are such as few travellers have written home, and yet fewer newspapers have elected to publish. James carries his mind with him; and though, in half-humorous deference to the catholicity of the public journal, he spares us any extended exposition of the 'Divine-natural Humanity,' he never ceases to be the social philosopher and political theorist. He neglects all which was most precious to the 'literary man' like his son Henry, in favor of inquiry into the state of society.

His letters record his horror of the European caste system, even as found in England. 'European institutions,' he writes, 'are based upon the sentiment not of human equality, but of human difference. They divide men into classes. . . . England seems to be completely fossilized by this monstrous fallacy. A friend of mine, and a man of distinction, told me the other day of a lady, one of his acquaintance, being obliged to take her boy from an excellent school, at which he had been attending for a couple of years, because the master had been indiscreet enough to take in a confectioner's

son.' And, horrible to relate, 'even liberal-minded men
here justify these monstrous wrongs. I have talked
with popular clergymen and literateurs on the subject, and they seem to have no idea of any organic
change in the social constitution of England being
desirable.' 'I give up the aristocratic institutions of
the country, whether secular or sacred, to your just
wrath, and would not move a finger to save the established Government or the established Church from
popular overthrow.'[3]

Yet in spite of English placidity, English indifference to the democratic movement, 'it seems inevitable
that revolution must one day ruffle these still waters
too. Only I could wish that it might normally grow
out of the felt exigencies of the people. . . . It is impossible that such an iniquitous distinction of classes
as exists here can continue much longer to affront
the great hope of man, the hope of social equality.'[4]

'The Social Significance of our Institutions,' which
Mr James delivered at Newport on the fourth of July
after his return to the States, leaves no doubt as to the
intensity of the lecturer's distaste for the European
spirit or his passionate loyalty to the American,—the
loyalty almost, so the flavor strikes one's palate, of a
convert, an immigrant.

Some paragraphs strongly intimate that the criticisms of American ways then as now freely published
by English travellers had irritated James. For his
part, he recalls English manners more distasteful to
him than any amount of indecorous Yankee freedom.

The stiff, polite chill which one has encountered among
the English proceeds, he feels, from lack of interest
in their fellows and a sense of caste prevailing acridly
over the sense of human brotherhood. Whatever the
crudity of American manners, the American heart
beats warmly, responds generously to the needs of all
mankind,—and that not merely in the abstract, but
in every most casual personal encounter.

'The intensely artificial structure of society in England renders it inevitable in fact, that her people should
be simply the worst-mannered people in Christendom.
Indeed, I venture to say that no average American
resides a year in England without getting a sense so
acute and stifling of its hideous class-distinctions, and
of the consequent awkwardness and *brusquerie* of its
upper classes, and the consequent abject snobbery or
inbred and ineradicable servility of its lower classes,
as makes the manners of Choctaws and Potawatamies
sweet and christian, and gives to a log-cabin in Oregon
the charm of comparative dignity and peace.' [5]

'I lived, recently, nearly a year in St John's Wood in
London, and was daily in the habit of riding down
to the City in the omnibus along with my immediate
neighbors, men of business and professional men. . . .
Very nice men, to use their own lingo, they were, for
the most part; tidy, unpretending, irreproachable in
dress and deportment; men in whose truth and honesty
you would confide at a glance; and yet, after eight
months' assiduous bosom solicitation of their hardened
stolid visages, I never was favored with the slightest

overture to human intercourse from one of them. I never once caught the eye of one of them. If ever I came nigh doing so, an instant film would surge up from their more vital parts, if such parts there were, just as a Newport fog suddenly surges up from the cold remorseless sea, and wrap the organ in the dullest, most disheartening of stares.'⁶

'And it is exactly the rebound of his thought from all this social obstruction and poverty which causes the American wayfarer's heart to dance with glee when he remembers his own incorrect and exceptionable Nazareth, his own benighted but comfortable and unsuspecting fellow-sinners, who are said to sit sometimes with their tired feet as high as their head, who light their innocent unconscious pipes at everybody's fire and who occasionally, when the sentiment of human brotherhood is at a white heat in their bosom, ask you, as a gentleman from Cape Cod once asked me at the Astor House table, the favor of being allowed to put his superfluous fat upon your plate, provided, that is, the fat is in no way offensive to you.'

Our loyalty to America reposes not upon its genteel manners but upon its spontaneous sense of human equality. Indeed, Mr James would say that what we cherish in America is her lack of gentility, her exuberant hospitality to all sorts and conditions of men.

'As Americans, we love our country, it is true, but not because it is *ours* simply; on the contrary, we are proud to belong to it, because it is the country of all mankind, because she opens her teeming lap to the exile of every land, and bares her hospitable breast to whatsoever wears the human form. This is where the ordinary European mind inevitably fails to do us any justice. The purblind piddling mercenaries of literature, like Dickens [Apparently the *American Notes* (1842) and *Martin Chuzzlewit* (1843) still rankled.] and the ominous scribes and Pharisees of the Saturday Review, have just enough of cheap wit to see and caricature the cordial complacency we feel in our beautiful and virgin mother. . . .'[7]

This state of mind was not in the least attributable to any personal grievance on James' part, for his own reception amongst the English had ever been most cordial, and that furthermore amongst the eminent of the day. It proceeded from all that was deepest in James' nature and all that was most central in his doctrine. In England, the moral life, the life which exalts personal claims over human, still prevailed; God's Divine Natural Humanity was still denied. In America, the democratic principle was already acknowledged in politics; the State Church had disappeared; a real society, in which God could fully become immanent, was approaching delivery.

II

James returned to America, doubtless cherishing illusions not a few about the public there awaiting his gospel—indulging, that is, an ill-warranted hope that his own country could by now provide him with some sort of intelligent comprehension. Illusion it chiefly proved: Mr James was all his life to find himself and his doctrine 'scantly enough heeded, reported or assimilated even in his own air, no brisk conductor at any time of his remarkable voice. . . .' None the less, Henry's judgment pronounces soundly: 'In Europe his isolation had been utter—he had there the sense of playing his mature and ardent thought over great dense constituted presences and opaque surfaces that could by their very nature scarce give back so much as a shudder . . . ; and I certainly came later on to rejoice in his having had after a certain date to walk, if there was a preference, rather in the thin wilderness than in the thick.' [8]

If disillusionment ensued, it did not amount to discouragement. There was the message, tremendous and imperative. If men did not heed, it was because the time was not yet ripe, or because the reporter was yet inadequate, groping, fumbling. The message itself one could not doubt; and loyalty to the cosmos demanded that one patiently proceed with one's reiteration.

The writing went on to the end. James' family found 'the sense of him, each long morning, at his study table either with bent considering brow or with a half-spent and checked intensity, a lapse backward in his chair and a musing lift of perhaps troubled and baffled eyes,' the most constant fact. 'He applied himself there with a regularity and a piety as little subject to sighing abatements or betrayed fears as if he had been working under pressure for his bread and ours and the question were too urgent for his daring to doubt.'⁹

There he sat at his desk, composing his papers as if the world were seriously eager for them, and revising and correcting as if a host of competent judges were to consider them. It is difficult to believe that he did not generally write rapidly and with fervor; but Henry recalls his now and then leaning back from his desk, 'again and again, in long fits of remoter consideration, wondering, pondering sessions into which I was more often than not moved to read . . . some story of acute inward difficulty amounting for the time to discouragement.'

He wrote facing the window, 'separated but by a pane of glass . . . from the general human condition he was so devoutly concerned with. He *saw* it, through the near glass, saw it in such detail and with such a feeling for it that it broke down nowhere—that was the great thing; which truth it confirmed that his very fallings back and long waits and stays and almost stricken musings witnessed exactly to his intensity, the intensity that would "come out," after all, and make his passionate philosophy and the fullest array of the appearances that couldn't be blinked fit together and harmonise.'¹⁰

His patient and inspired work brought him 'throughout the long years no ghost of a reward in the form of pence, and could proceed to publicity, as it repeatedly did, not only by the copious and resigned sacrifice of such calculations, but by his meeting in every single case all the expenses of the process.'[11]

The books met small understanding. A few reviewers, James Freeman Clarke, George Howison, C. S. Peirce, Mrs Orr in the *Athenæum*, took the trouble to read painstakingly and sympathetically.[12] Few real disciples made themselves known, though these few, chiefly women, gave him really intelligent hearing and thereby much comfort: his correspondence with them was, William thinks, 'perhaps his principal solace and recreation.'[13] Some of these voluble correspondences survive, notably that which Julia Kellogg, whose *Philosophy of Henry James* attests to her understanding of her friend.[14] They exhibit the same range of interests as the books, the same rich style, the same pungent blend of the most abstract thought with most personal idiom. Indeed, with James the essay and the letter were never quite distinguished; *Christianity the Logic of Creation* and *Society the Redeemed Form of Man* both constitute series of letters printed with much of their informal fluency still upon them; and the unpublished letter ever strains toward the essay.

That James was not impervious to the almost total silence which received his efforts comes out touchingly enough in a letter he wrote an appreciative reader named Barr: 'I am thankful to hear from you that some good resulted to you intellectually from our correspondence: thankful as well as *surprised*. I have always had a great good will to the truth, but somehow my intelligence has poorly seconded my good

will, else I should not have been so fruitless a writer.'[15]
He concludes with a hope which has already in some
measure been realized: 'Perhaps however my books
may find readers at a later period.'

III

In his later years—that is, after his removal to Cambridge—James moved in the best literary society of
the day. He was promptly voted a member of the
Saturday Club, that distinguished group which monthly
convened at the Parker House. He frequented the
salon of Mrs Fields. In the 'seventies, he was a member of the Chestnut Street Radical Club.[16]

The mood of the 1840's, its eager welcome to reform, to advanced social thought, to theological icono-
clasm, had passed; and for all James had never been
more than a purely speculative as well as altogether
urbane and civilized reformer, he lived on into a world
which found him essentially a survival.

Echoes linger on of James' bearing in this society,
his witty, paradoxical conversation, his color as a 'character.' He carried freely into public his domestic
habit of saying whatever would cause a shock and
hence excite some sort of spirited reaction. With
abundant social tact and plenty of shrewd knowledge of
men, he did not always choose to adapt himself or
his remarks to the company in which he found himself,
but delivered himself copiously, explosively, as the
spirit or a sense of mischief might move,

Henry recalls his 'finely contentious or genially perverse impulse to carry his wares of observation to the
market in which they would on the whole bring least
rather than most—where his offering them at all would
produce rather a flurry (there might have been markets
in which it had been known to produce almost a
scandal). . . .'[17]

Frank Sanborn relates a much-told anecdote in which
James characteristically figures. Bronson Alcott was
holding a 'conversation' in Emerson's parlor at Concord, with Emerson's aunt, Thoreau, Sanborn, and
James among the company. 'Not understanding the
law of an Alcottian conversation, [James] began and
continued to show his own wit by perplexing the subject with some of his questions and witty paradoxes.
. . . Alcott fell into polite silence, and Thoreau, while
contesting some of James' assumptions, could not check
the flow of the semi-Hibernian rhetoric,—in which,
as Thoreau said afterward, James uttered "*quasi* philanthropic doctrines in a metaphysical dress, but for all
the practical purposes very crudely, charging society
with all the crime committed, and praising the crimi-
nal for committing it." Miss [Mary Moody] Emerson
heard this with rising wrath; but when, finally, James
spoke repeatedly and scornfully of the Moral Law,
her patience gave way. Rising from her chair . . .
[she] began her answer to these doctrines of Satan,
as she thought them. She expressed her amazement
that any man should denounce the Moral Law,—the
only tie of society, except religion, to which, she saw,

the speaker made no claim. She referred him to his Bible and to Dr Adam Clarke (one of her great authorities from childhood,) and she denounced him personally in the most racy terms. She did not cross the room and shake him, as one reporter, not an eye-witness, has fancied,—but she retained her position, sat down quietly when she had finished, and was complimented by the smiling James. . . .' [18]

His *obiter dicta,* as reported by the memoir writers of the period, are everywhere characteristic. Fields inquires who wrote the review of *Substance and Shadow* for the *Examiner.* 'Oh! that was *merely* Freeman Clarke,' James answers; 'he is a smuggler in theology and feels towards me much as a contraband towards an exciseman.' He warns the company not to expect reason from Carlyle, who is 'an artist, a wilful artist, and no reasoner. He has only genius.' [19]

On another occasion he 'had gone so far as to abuse Emerson pretty well [on purely 'spiritual' grounds, surely] when the latter came in. "How do you do, Emer-son," he said, with his peculiar intonation and voice, as if he had expected him on the heels of what had gone before.' In Mr Alcott, he pronounced on yet another occasion, 'the moral sense was wholly dead, and the æsthetic sense had never been born.' [20]

Familiar doctrines as well as persons recur: 'He anticipates a change in European affairs; the age of ignorance is to pass away and strong democratic tendencies will soon pervade Europe. The march of civilization will work its revenge against aristocratic England, he believes.' 'He said society was to blame for much [*much* is moderate language for James] of the crime in it, and as for that poor young man who committed the murder at Malden, it was a mere fact of temperament or inheritance.' [21]

Occasionally, James still read a lecture. In 1868 the New England Women's Club announced a course 'at which articles of interest are expected from Mr R. W. Emerson, Mrs Julia Ward Howe, Mr Henry James, and other distinguished literary persons.' He appeared twice before the Radical Club (the center, in the 'seventies, for the latter-day Transcendentalists), discoursing on 'Nature and Person' and 'Marriage.'

At the request of the ladies of Cambridge, he enunciated his views on 'Woman.' But twenty persons convened to hear him, those chiefly churchmen. True to his convictions, James 'didn't fail to whip the "pusillanimous" clergy,' and, writes Mrs Field, 'as the room was overstocked with them, it was odd to watch the effect. Mr James is perfectly brave, almost inapprehensive of the storm of opinion he raises. . . .'

Once at least he occupied a pulpit—that of Dr Freeman Clarke's Church of the Disciples. Again he bore witness to the faith that was in him, denouncing the Church and the moral law as the meanest of inventions. Mrs Howe and her children sat among his auditors; and her sixteen year old daughter comprehended enough of the diatribe against Phariseeism to burst out, after service, with: 'Mamma, I should think that Mr James would wish the little Jameses not to

wash their faces for fear it should make them suppose
that they were clean'—a comment which is said to
have elicited Emerson's hearty laugh.[22]

IV

In his last years, Mr James doubtless came to be remembered by the world at large, if remembered he
was, rather for his associations with Emerson and
Carlyle and his other illustrious friends, and as the
father of two gifted sons, than in his own right. The
intelligent reporter for the Boston *Sunday Herald*
who interviewed Mr James a few years before his
death, the obituaries which appeared in the *Transcript,*
the *Nation,* and elsewhere all convey this impression.[23]

The *Herald* reporter, who found Mr James among
the 'notable people who frequent the "Old Corner"
[bookshop] in Boston to see the most recent book from
England, to hear the latest literary gossip or seek a
chance interview with a friend,' does indeed give a
full and intelligent resumé of James' intellectual history and his philosophy, but he devotes most space to
the elderly sage's reminiscences of his eminent contemporaries; and the impression that the reporter really
came in search of precisely that is confirmed by Mr
James' letters to the *Herald:* 'Your reporter began the
conversation by asking me to tell him what I knew
about Carlyle.'[24]

About Carlyle and Emerson, his two most illustrious friends, there was much desire to hear. In his

last years James took advantage of the public's fancy by writing lectures on both of them.[25] No doubt the public desired literary gossip; but it got, instead, most characteristic criticisms of the men and their doctrines and their position in relation to human society, outspoken and audacious estimates of venerated names.

James' consistent later view of Carlyle represents him as compounded of prejudice and rhetoric,—rhetoric sometimes in the service of prejudice, sometimes an end in itself.

In substance, there are two indictments: Carlyle lacked any genuine belief in humanity; he believed in heroes, not in men. In terms of Mr James' favorite distinction, he was 'deficient in spiritual as opposed to moral force.' 'In the teeth of all the prophets who have ever prophesied, he held that the race *is* always to the swift, the battle always to the strong. Long before Mr Darwin had thought of applying the principle of natural selection to the animal kingdom, Carlyle, not in words but in fact, had applied it to the spiritual Kingdom, proclaiming it as fundamental axiom of the divine administration.'

'He had no belief in society as a living, organizing force, in history, but only as an empirical necessity of the race.'[26] He believed in the finality of the conflict between good and evil; found the conflict valid in itself, its own end; never guessed that it was merely propadeutic to an ultimate and permanent harmony.

But worse, he was a literary man before everything

else, and essentially subordinated even the ignoble doctrine he preached to the exigencies of his personal genius. 'Carlyle was, in truth, a hardened declaimer. He talked in a way vastly to tickle his auditors, and his enjoyment of their amusement was lively enough to sap his own intellectual integrity. Artist like, he precipitated himself upon the picturesque in character and manners wherever he found them, and he did not care a jot what incidental interest his precipitancy lacerated.'

'You would say, remembering certain passages in Carlyle's books,—notably his "Past and Present" and his pamphlet on Chartism,—that he had a very lively sympathy with reform and a profound sentiment of human fellowship. He did, indeed, dally with the divine ideas long enough to suck them dry of their rhetorical juices, but then dropped them, to lavish contempt on them ever after when anybody else should chance to pick them up and cherish them, not for their rhetorical uses, but their absolute truth.' [27]

J. T. Fields thought James' article on Carlyle 'too abusive, especially as he stayed in his house, or was there long and familiarly.' Yet he does not attribute the abuse to any baser motive than patriotism: James' 'love of country was bitterly stung by Carlyle in "Shooting Niagara and After," ' which appeared in 1867. [28]

Doubtless James was hurt, as were many of Carlyle's American readers, by 'Shooting Niagara'; [29] but James' attitude toward Carlyle quite antedates the article; James had written a rather merciless review of the *Frederick* for the *Nation* in 1865;[30] and indeed an appendix to *Christianity the Logic of Creation* (1857) falls not far short.

James could not forgive Carlyle his glorification of the hero, his contempt for democracy, his denial of the Divine Natural Humanity. And if there is more of a note of bitterness in the pages upon Carlyle than James elsewhere allows himself, it sounds his disappointment at a 'lost leader,' an idealist who has sunk into a rhetorician, who has turned sour.

V

Emerson remained the puzzle he had ever been: at once irritation and enchantment; intellectually sterile, personally altogether winsome and prophetic of the coming man, the man of destiny and immemorial promise. 'Mr Emerson's authority to the imagination consists, not in his culture, not in his science, but all simply in himself, in the form of his natural personality. There are scores of men of more advanced ideas than Mr Emerson, of subtler apprehension, of broader knowledge, of deeper culture. . . . Mr Emerson was never the least of a pedagogue, addressing your scientific intelligence, but an every way unconscious prophet, appealing exclusively to the regenerate heart of mankind, and announcing the speedy fulfilment of the hope with which it had always been pregnant. He was an American John the Baptist, proclaiming tidings

of great joy to the American Israel; but, like John
the Baptist, he could so little foretell the form in which
the predicted good was to appear, that when you went
to him he was always uncertain whether you were
he who should come, or another.'

James was not in the least disposed, in the fashion
of Arnold, to deny the Concordian the eminence of
great writer. 'There is no technical man of letters in
the land who will not cordially bow to Mr Emerson's
literary sceptre . . .' Emerson's 'speech is colour and
melody and fragrance itself to my senses' . . . Yet he
will agree with Arnold that his preëminence lay elsewhere. 'I think it has never once occurred to me in
my long intercourse with Mr Emerson to prize his
literary friendship, or covet any advantage which
might accrue from it to myself. No, what alone I have
sought in Mr Emerson is not the conscious scholar, but
always the unconscious prophet, whose genius, and
not by any means his intellect, announces, with un-
precedented emphasis, spontaneity as the supreme law
of human life.'

Not for what he thought or said or wrote but for
what he was and what he adumbrated could James
be grateful. One could turn from his thought to his
character, all innocent of moralism, all spontaneous,
all instinct with the Divine: there one found satisfaction. His thought, like the thought of all the Transcendentalists, exalted individualism; his spirit exhibited the sweetest graces of a universal humanity.

Though Emerson, like Carlyle, has a veneration for

the great, there is this profound difference in their attitude: that Carlyle makes of them heroes, set apart by their genius from our common humanity; Emerson makes of them *representative* men. 'He indeed honours great men, but only for their human substance . . . ; they *do* represent something more than they individually constitute, and this is a great gain.'

Carlyle, unknowingly, ends the old moralistic dispensation; Emerson, with equal unconsciousness, inaugurates the new. He 'rings in that better world inaugurated by the second Adam, in which at last the divine spirit is supreme, and our nature, consequently touched by that inspiration, brings forth immaculate fruit; that is, all those spontaneous graces of heart and mind and manners which alone have power to redeem us to eternal innocence, peace, and self-oblivion.' [31]

This estimate of Emerson, composed in 1868 or thereabouts, underwent no substantial alteration in what William James calls 'a more unceremonious view' of the subject,[32] that given in a chapter of *Spiritual Creation* (1882). Mr James indeed here pretends to a grievance in finding 'my recently deceased friend Mr Emerson . . . all his days an arch traitor to our existing civilized regimen, inasmuch as he unconsciously managed to set aside its fundamental principle in doing without conscience . . .', or, as he yet more strikingly puts it: Emerson 'never felt a movement of the life of conscience from the day of his birth till that of his death.' [33] But Mr James had his own way

with language. *Civilization* was a pejorative term and
meant to him, as to Fourier, the present moralistic-
capitalistic order, viewed as now nearing its end. And
conscience is of course the mark and sign of the moral
order. Emerson anticipated—and that the miracle of
him—the coming social order, in which conscience
would be swallowed up in love, as self-consciousness
in spontaneity.

And the positive testimony remains substantially
the same. The main thing about his was that he 'unconsciously brought you face to face with the infinite
in humanity . . .' Everything in him 'seemed innocent
by the transparent absence of selfhood . . .' He 'recognized no God outside of himself and his interlocutor,
and recognized him there only as the *liaison* between
the two, taking care that all their intercourse should
be holy with a holiness undreamed of before by man
or angel. For it is not a holiness taught by books or
the example of tiresome, diseased, self-conscious saints,
but simply by one's own redeemed flesh and blood.'
The holiness for which Emerson lived was innocence;
and innocence 'attaches only to what is definitely
universal or natural in our experience, and hence ap-
propriates itself to individuals only in so far as they
learn to denude themselves of personality or self-
consciousness . . .'[34]

James' *obiter dicta* upon his other literary friends
possess the same freshness and downright frankness.
With their strictly literary work, he cannot of course
bother. Without denying its merit or even doubting

it, he is ever impatient of what, to him, is purely mediatory or vehicular; he is concerned with the man and his ideas.[35]

In a letter written after a meeting of the Saturday Club he tellingly records his impressions of his companions. 'Hawthorne isn't to me a prepossessing figure, nor apparently at all an *enjoying* person in any way: he has all the while the look—or would have to the unknowing—of a rogue who suddenly finds himself in a company of detectives. But in spite of his rusticity I felt a sympathy for him fairly amounting to anguish . . . The thing was that Hawthorne seemed to me to possess human substance and not to have dissipated it all away like that culturally debauched——, or even like good inoffensive comforting Longfellow. . . . W. Ellery Channing too seemed so human and good—sweet as summer and fragrant as pinewoods. He is more sophisticated than Hawthorne of course, but still he was kin; and I felt the world richer by two *men,* who had not yet lost themselves in mere members of society.'[36]

Thoreau, James confided to the columns of the *Sunday Herald,* 'was literally the most childlike, unconscious and unblushing egotist it has ever been my fortune to encounter in the ranks of manhood; so that, if he happened to visit you on a Sunday morning, when possibly you were in a devout frame of mind, as like as not you would soon find yourself intoning subaudible praises to the meticulous skill which had at last succeeded in visibly marrying such sheer and mountainous inward self-esteem with such harmless and beautiful force of outward demeanor. I have not had the advantage, to be sure, of knowing Thoreau well, through the medium of his books, which so many competent persons praise as singularly witty and sagacious. I have, however, honestly tried to read them, but owing, I suppose, to prejudice derived from personal contact with him, their wit always seemed more or less spoiled, to my taste, by intention, and even their sagacity seemed painfully aggressive and alarming; so I relinquished my task without any edifying result.' [87]

VI

If James expressed himself with some frankness about his associates, no one would suspect him of jealousy. His largeness of nature forbade any bitterness over the difference between the size of his audience and that which attended Emerson and Carlyle. And never thinking of himself (as indeed he had no necessity) as the inferior of his more famous friends, he had no desire to abase their reputations that his own might be exalted.

His untempered criticism was motivated partly by sincere dissent from the philosophies they represented (Transcendental individualism and Carlylian hero worship, alike offensive to a democrat), partly, perhaps principally, from the desire to rebuke the wide-spread taste for literary gossip and the wide-spread veneration for great names. How could men worship God's

incarnation in society when they forever retailed anecdotes and *obiter dicta* of fashionable men of letters?
To magnify personalities is to make light of God's
redemptive work in humanity.

'Nothing so endlessly besotted in Mr James' eyes,'
writes William, 'as the pretension to possess personally
any substantive merit or advantage whatever, any
worth other than your unconscious uses to your kind!
Nothing pleased him like exploding the bubbles of
conventional dignity, unless it was fraternizing on the
simplest and lowest plane with all lowly persons
whom he met.' [38]

He wrote Miss Kellogg: [39] "The common place people
you despise in comparison with Plato and Emerson
are not agreeable to me on the score of any spiritual
attainments they appear to have made, but only on the
ground of their not exhibiting so dense an obscuration
in their proper personality, of the Divine glory. They
seem to be immersed in active use, to cherish no consciousness of virtue or genius or talent or anything
of that sort, and so let the Lord shine through them
without any excessive clouding of his splendour. But
your Platos and Emersons are somebodies in respect
to these nobodies, and I accordingly who live only
by trying to believe in the Lord's sole worth in humanity, and am therefore delighted always to be with
self-evident nobodies, feel greatly discontented and
disheartened to find that I have to deal also with these
pretentious somebodies and dispose of them before
I can again get a sight of the Lord. . . . Whenever I

get my stupid sconce above water for half an hour, some of the reigning idols, Plato or Emerson or Washington, is sure to plump himself down upon it, and submerge me in the atheistic flood for another century. The people in the horse-cars never do this. They never stimulate me to show off. They never suggest to me that there [are] differences among men in themselves. . . . They talk so heartily of household expenses and weather and raising chickens that it is sweet to be near them.'

The horse-car became at once a shrine and a symbol to James. His friend Godkin, editor of the *Nation,* quotes him as maintaining that to a right-minded man a crowded Cambridge horse-car 'was the nearest approach to Heaven on earth.'[40]

In *Society the Redeemed Form of Man,*[41] James pays his devotions at the same shrine. Under the grand heading 'The Horse-Car our True Shechinah at This Day,' he confesses to the 'frankly chaotic or *a-*cosmical aspect of our ordinary street-car' only to avow: 'I nevertheless continually witness so much mutual forbearance on the part of its *habitués;* so much spotless acquiescence under the rudest personal jostling and inconvenience; such a cheerful renunciation of one's strict right; such an amused deference, oftentimes, to one's invasive neighbor: in short, and as a general thing, such a heavenly self-shrinkage in order that "the neighbor," handsome or unhandsome, wholesome or unwholesome, may sit or stand at ease: that I not seldom find myself inwardly exclaiming with the patriarch: *How dreadful is this place! It is none other than the house of God, and the gate of heaven!'*

VII

Mrs James died in February 1882. Her husband survived her only till December. His strength had been gradually weakening for some time; and his 'general mental powers were visibly altered' during the last year, but not so his grasp of his philosophy. 'His truths were his life; and when all else had ebbed away, his grasp of them was still vigorous and sure.' During those last months he busied himself correcting the proofs of his *Spiritual Creation*,[42] much of which had appeared, after his favorite epistolary fashion, in the *New-Church Independent*.

In October he wrote his old friend Godwin: 'The making of the book has been my only refuge against the suffering involved in the loss of my wife. . . . For four or five months I didn't see how I was going to live without her. I had actually run down to death's door when we moved to the country, and I have been slowly pulling up since. But even now I am miserably feeble, and look forward to nothing with so much desire as to a reunion beyond the skies with my adorable wife.'[43]

The end came too suddenly for either Henry or William, both abroad, to reach home in time. Henry, who started for America immediately upon receiving intimation of his father's serious illness, arrived the night after the funeral. He sent William an account of the last days:

'Father had been so tranquil, so painless, had died so easily and, as it were deliberately. . . . He simply, after the "improvement" of which we were written before I sailed, had a sudden relapse—a series of swoons—after which he took to his bed not to rise again. He had no visible malady—strange as it may seem. The "softening of the brain" was simply a gradual refusal of food, because he *wished* to die. There was no dementia except a sort of exaltation of his belief that he had entered into "the spiritual life." Nothing could persuade him to eat, and yet he never suffered, or gave the least sign of suffering, from inanition. . . . He prayed and longed to die. He ebbed and faded away, though in spite of his strength becoming continually less, he was able to see people and talk. He wished to see as many people as he could, and he talked with them without effort. . . . Alice says he said the most picturesque and humorous things. He knew I was coming and was glad, but not impatient. . . . He had no belief apparently that he should live to see me, but was perfectly cheerful about it. He slept a great deal, and . . . there was "so little of the sick-room" about him. He lay facing the windows, which he would never have darkened—never pained by the light . . .'⁴⁴

A week before he died, his daughter asked for directions about his funeral. 'He was immediately very much interested, not having apparently thought of it before; he reflected for some time, and then said with the greatest solemnity and looking so majestic: "Tell him to say only this: 'Here lies a man, who has thought all his life that the ceremonies attending birth, marriage and death were all damned non-sense.' Don't let him say a word more." ' [45]

Among his last utterances [46] was the declaration of unwavering belief in the Divine, with the fullest disowning of self: 'I stick by Almighty God—He alone *is*, all else is death. Don't call this dying; I am just entering upon life.'

CHAPTER VIII

THE PHILOSOPHY

'WHENEVER the eye falls upon one of Mr James' pages,
—whether it be a letter to a newspaper or to a friend,
whether it be his earliest or his latest book,—we seem
to find him saying again and again the same thing;
telling us what the true relation is between mankind
and its Creator. What he had to say on this point was
the burden of his whole life, and its only burden. When
he had said it once, he was disgusted with the insufficiency of the formulation (he always hated the
sight of his old books), and set himself to work to
say it again. But he never analysed his terms or his
data beyond a certain point, and made very few fun-
damentally new discriminations; so the result of all
these successive re-editings was repetition and amplifi-
cation and enrichment, rather than reconstruction.
The student of any one of his works knows, consequently, all that is *essential* in the rest.'[1]

A young author's first book must compress between

its covers a complete transcription of his experience and his theories. James never outgrew this adolescent prodigality. Besides his reading of the secret of the universe, he was possessed of views upon a range of lesser themes: crime, poverty, wealth, waste; marriage and the 'woman question'; Swedenborg and the Swedenborgians; spiritualism; art; metaphysics. Instead of devoting a book to each of his interests, he devotes every book to all of them, runs the full gamut upon every occasion. This is largely true even of his appearances in magazines. Whatever the announced topic (Woman, Crime, Spiritualism), we presently find ourselves running precipitously into the theory of Creation.

James' earlier writings were largely occupied with negative criticisms of religious orthodoxy, both Evangelical and Swedenborgian.[2] The later works never weary of defining their position by its contrariety to current views in philosophy and science as well as religion. But combat is not their *raison d'être*. Their 'superficial polemics' never disturb the central peace which pervades them.[3]

James published four full-length portraitures of his mind: *Christianity the Logic of Creation* (1857), *Substance and Shadow* (1863), *The Secret of Swedenborg* (1869), *Society the Redeemed Form of Man* (1879); and during the last year of his life he was revising the proof of a fifth, *Spiritual Creation* (1882). The first of these is the most succinct; but the later formulations are not only, as William James thought, philosophically the best, but the best written as well. 'Best' for both philosophy and style must be interpreted *most characteristic of James*. James indeed disliked any dwelling upon the personal and wanted to enunciate what was true not for him but for all men: of no philosopher could this appeal to the universal be more forcibly urged. Yet his whole turn of mind and his intensely vivid and individual idiom set him apart from both the philosophers and the men of letters of his day. He was too much of a dialectician to turn *littérateur*, but he balked at limiting himself to ratiocination. He argues; and wearying of argument, he turns to striking example, pungent satire, eloquent apostrophe, prophetic declaration. For all his fond addiction to verbal distinctions, he uses his terms freely, not exactly, not consistently.

Mr James' style at his most characteristic deserves the high praise which has so abundantly been awarded it,[4] not for organization—that James lacked, was impatient of; but for style in the romantic sense: for diction by turns learned and homely, incomparably varied and rich and living; sentences sharpened to aphorism; paragraphs which work to a climax; longer sequences in which the author feels emotionally moved by his own argument and loses himself in the poetry of it. Wit and passion glow by turns.

A writer of passages James is, rather than a writer of books; just as he is by turns the reasoner, but always the prophet and seer.

Best, as thus defined—that is, most characteristic of

their author, most rich in the display of his powers of humor, eloquence, perception—are *The Secret of Swedenborg, Society the Redeemed Form of Man* and *Spiritual Creation.* Grand books these: America has produced nothing else like them; but Mark Twain, Melville, and Whitman, rather than Emerson or Hawthorne, are their parallels for virility of spirit and robustness of expression.

I

And now to come to the philosophy itself, it must first be inquired how we apprehend truth, as distinguished from sense perception and 'fact.' Suppose (in Swedenborgian language) that God is pleased to call his children out of Egypt, and its 'scientifics,' its memory-knowledge, into the Promised Land of spiritual wisdom: how will he effect it?

Not by theology, with its myth and dogma; not by metaphysics, with its ratiocination *(God is not pleased to save his people by dialectic)*; not by Science, with its limitation to fact and phenomena, James answers, but by Philosophy.

Philosophy—true philosophy, that is—operates by perception, intuition. It attends to the voice of the heart; to race instinct, vaguer and deeper yet; to *the hidden God.*

'Science confines herself only to phenomena and their relations, that is, to what is strictly verifiable in some sort by sense; and so stigmatizes the pursuit

of being or substance as fatal to her fundamental principles. Philosophy, in short, is the pursuit of Truth,
supersensuous truth, recognisable only by the heart of
the race, or if by its intellect, still only through a life
and power derived from the heart. Science has no eye
for truth, but only for Fact, which is the appearance
that truth puts on to the senses, and is therefore intrinsically second-hand, or shallow and reflective.'

'Ratiocination is doubtless an honest pastime, or it
would not be so much in vogue as a means of ac-
quiring truth. But the truth we are elucidating is
Divine, and therefore is great enough to authenticate
itself, or furnish its own evidence.'

'I shall not affront your self-respect,' James assures
us, 'by affecting to demonstrate the truth of God's
NATURAL humanity scientifically: in the first place,
because it is not a fact of sense, and therefore escapes
the supervision of science; and in the second place,
because . . . I am anxious to conciliate your heart
primarily, while your head is quite a subordinate aim.
I cannot tell you a single reason, unprompted by the
heart, why I myself believe the truth in question or
any other truth for that matter. . . . In fact, I believe
it simply because I love it, or it seems adorably good
to me; and once having learned to love it, I could
not do without it. It would in truth kill me, intellectually, to doubt it. . . . To my experience this is the
only thing that in the long run authenticates truth
to the intellect—*the heart's sincere craving for it.* I
find that truth unloved is always at bottom truth

unbelieved, however much it may be "professed." ' [5]

Sometimes James calls this philosophy of the heart Revelation. His point in appropriating this term is to underscore the self-evident, primary character of religious intuition; to distinguish it from other sorts of knowledge which are derivative from sense perception. It may be true of the intellect that it contains nothing which was not first in the senses; but it is distinctly not true of the soul. James scorns the orthodox notion of Revelation, which makes it to consist in deliverances of alleged historical occurrences and legal precepts.

Revelation conveys to us first principles which neither observation nor experience nor the reasonings thence derived could possibly warrant. There would be no object in the *revelation* of truth which could be arrived at empirically and verified by experiment. *Credo quia impossible:* it is in that sort of truth that Revelation deals. The deepest aspirations of the heart seem so palpably beyond our experience actual or possible as to disavow all phenomenal parentage. 'Flesh and blood hath not revealed it unto you:' that much we feel sure of. The 'supremely true is never the probable. . . .' 'The sphere of Revelation is the sphere of life exclusively, and its truth is addressed not to the reflective understanding of men, but to their living perception. Truth, to every soul that has ever felt its inward breathing, disowns all outward authority,—disowns, if need be, all outward *probability* or attestation of Fact. The only witness it craves, and this witness it depends upon, is that of good in the heart.' [6]

About 'revelation' we cannot of course argue. It is primary and self-evident,—its own witness. We can merely avow it, and let it make its way into the hearts of all sincere and spiritual persons to whose attention it may come.

The 'precious facts of revelation, whether they fall within the sphere of my understanding or my affections, quite transcend the grasp of my critical faculty, and impose themselves upon my heart as an unmixed good, which I am just as incapable of measuring in terms of the analytic intellect, or reducing to the contrast of the true and the false, as I am of demonstrating to a blind man the pleasure of a gorgeous sunset, or reasoning a man without a palate into the savor of sugar.'[7]

II

So much for James' theory of knowledge.

His philosophy may be called one of *Creation,* provided we are willing to give the term an ontological rather than a cosmological flavor. By this favorite word of his, James was far from meaning the process whereby Jehovah's *fiat* brought into time and space existence the natural world; and he was not in the least troubled over the early narrative of Genesis and whether the 'six days' were twenty-four hours or an aeon in duration. Evolution was, to him, quite conceivable as a scientific hypothesis, and as such could in no way conflict with a philosophic theory of creation.

It provokes James to vehemence that scientists and

theologians alike take Nature as primary and ultimate, as a real creature. Nature is the least real of all existences, for nature is 'a mere implication of man, . . . exists *in itself* only to carnal thought, or an intelligence unemancipated from sense. . . .' All that sensibly exists is 'but the mind's furniture.' The spiritual thought of man 'makes all sensible existence to fall within the unitary mind of the race. . . .'

Nature exists not in the least in her own right, is indeed completely void of substance. Her existence is strictly dependent upon humanity. Natural phenomena have 'no other function than outwardly to image or represent the things of human affection and thought, which alone make up the spiritual creation, or are alone objective to the divine mind.'[8]

The relation of Nature to man requires further explication. Nature indeed mirrors the race mind; but at the same time Nature is necessary to the mind of the individual man. Consciousness sets man off from his creator; Nature gives that consciousness the only possible ground for operation.

By imaging forth spiritual verities, natural objects acquaint the spirit of man with his own constitution. If my sensible experience 'did not furnish my rational understanding with a complete livery or symbolism of abstract human nature, with an infinitely modulated key wherewith to unlock all the secret chambers of the human heart, all the infinite possibilities of character among men—I should be forever destitute of moral perception . . .; because thought is impossible without language; and language derives all its substance or body from things, or the contents of our sensible experience.'[9]

The true creature of God is man. God's essence is Love; as Swedenborg asserts in *Sapientia Angelica,* 'This is love, that one's own should be another's. . . . Conjunction of love is the result of reciprocity; and reciprocity can have no place in one person only. If it is thought possible it is merely imaginary. It is clear therefore that the Divine Love cannot but be and exist in others whom it may love, and by whom it may be loved. For since such a principle is in all love, it must be specially, that is, infinitely, in Love Itself.

'As for God, it is impossible for Him to love and to be loved reciprocally in others having anything of infinity, that is, anything of the essence and life of love in itself, or anything of the Divine.' In such case, God would be loving himself, for there is but one Divine Substance, one Very Reality. And of self-love, Swedenborg tells us, 'there cannot be the least trace in God, for it is altogether opposed to the Divine Essence.'[10]

The real creation is the creation of creatures whom God may love. God alone is Life, and he cannot create other beings having life in themselves. Yet he must in some sense project his creatures off from himself, give them if not *being,* then at least *existence.* That the creatures should be real as God is real flouts every philosophic instinct, but they must possess at the

least a sort of reality, a quasi-reality, a reality to themselves, else there is no escape from Pantheism, and
God is loving not others but himself.

Sometimes James gives the name of creation only
to the process whereby God projects us from himself;
sometimes he makes it cover as well the return, the
redemption, as he elsewhere calls it. Thus he says in
the *Secret,* 'creation, philosophically viewed, involves
a divided movement—one descending, generic, physical, by which the creature becomes set off, projected,
alienated from the creator in mineral, vegetable, and
animal form; the other ascending, specific, moral, by
which the creature thus pronounced becomes *conscious of himself* as separated from his creative source,
and instinctively reacts against the fact, or seeks to
reunite himself with God.' [11]

III

Creation as projection. How is God to set the
creature off from himself without on the one hand
making him objectively disjunct, real as God is real;
or on the other reducing him to the mere appearance
of Reality?

Taking a hint from Swedenborg, James declares
that God can at most afford man only a provisional
reality; man is not to possess life in himself, but merely
to feel as if he possessed life in himself. He really lives
in God, but he is to suppose himself acting and living
'as of himself.'

Is the self, then, purely illusory? Swedenborg does
not help us to interpret this doctrine of the provisional
self. James does. He asserts that we have to deal
with two orders, two 'discrete degrees,' of the real.
The self is illusory only from an absolute or philosophic
point of view; but just as nature is *real* to the senses
(illusory only when taken philosophically as ·possess-
ing substance), so with the self: that is real on its
own plane—that is, to consciousness.

Man, '*in so far as he is man,* does not exist to sense,
but only to consciousness, and consequently human
nature properly speaking is not a thing of physical
but of strictly moral attributes. In so far as man exists
to sense he is identical with mineral, vegetable and
animal; and it is only as he exists to consciousness, that
he becomes naturally differentiated or individualized
from these lower forms, and puts on a truly human,
which is an exclusively moral, personality.' [12]

James over and over distinguishes Creator from
created as Substance from Form, Essence from Existence. God is our *Esse,* as we are his *Existere.* In
the language of post-Kantian philosophy, our objectivity
rests in God, while he attains to subjectivity (is this
what the Christian doctrine of the Incarnation means?)
only in us.

God neither possesses consciousness nor can be possessed by it. Human consciousness, indeed, is the wall
between us and God, erected by God in order to give
us a room of our own; and the wall hides us from
our benefactor.

In giving us this consciousness from which he is hidden, this 'proud and sufficient selfhood' whereby man may 'absolutely deny his maker, and search the universe in vain to find a God' . . . , God truly creates, and how truly and completely! No legerdemain will suffice, no 'brisk activity.' The Incarnation of God in man, and through man to ultimate nature, is, indeed, rather to be thought of as patient suffering, as self-emptying. God took upon him the form of a servant, not merely in Jesus, but in his whole creative work. Creation is 'no ostentatious self-assertion, no dazzling parade of magical, irrational, or irresponsible power; it is an endless humiliation or prorogation of [God] himself to all the lowest exigencies of the created consciousness.' [13]

God indeed so completely abases himself, so veils his splendor from consciousness, so fears to break in upon the selfhood of his creatures, that he runs the risk of their confirming themselves in their first and perfectly natural thought that they really are, what they seem to themselves to be, self-sufficient.

'The palpable logic of creation—considered as an exact equation between the creative fulness and the created want—is that the former be utterly swallowed up by the latter, or actually disappear within its boundless stomach. In other words, in order to the creature coming to self-consciousness, or getting projection from the creator, it is necessary that the latter actually pass over to the created nature, cheerfully assume and eternally bear the lineaments of its abysmal destitution:

so that practically, or in its initiament, creation takes on a wholly illusory aspect, the creature alone appearing, and the creator consequently reduced to actual non-existence, or claiming at most a traditional recognition.'[14]

Evil indeed comes into being along with the self. Not indeed that the self in itself is evil: in itself it is the necessary platform for all man's subsequent moral and spiritual development. But not to recognize this, its provisional character, to confirm oneself in the belief that it is as absolute as it appears, is to fall into evil.

'The original sin of the creature—his $\pi\rho\omega\tau o\eta$ $\psi\epsilon\upsilon\delta o\varsigma$ from which all his evils and falses flow—is that he feels himself to exist *absolutely;* and this is a sin he may well be unconscious of, since the boundless love of his creator is at the bottom of it. At least if God gave himself to his creature in a finite manner, there could be no danger of the sin being committed. But He gives himself to the creature without stint, in *infinite* measure; and the creature cannot help feeling therefore that he is life in himself.'[15]

IV

Here, then, is man projected from God, given what possible degree of otherness God can assign him. How, now, does the return movement effect itself? How does man reconcile himself with his creator? They have been made two on purpose that union may result, that they may be one, not by identity but by mutual love.

James found two answers more or less generally accepted in his day: moralism and ecclesiasticism; both he rejected as false, the more so for their arrogant pretensions to tremendous rightness. 'Who are Christ's spiritual foes, the only foes possible to him at this day? They are *friends . . . to his carnal or historic personality.* The first class may be for convenience sake called moralistic: being made up of that very large number of persons who live and thrive in contentment with the existing very infirm constitution of society: poets, literary essayists, scholars, artists, *transcendental aspirants or idealists* [italics mine], men of science . . . : all of whom blindly regard morality as the absolute law of human life, and look upon duty as the highest expression of human character, especially for other people.

'The second class is mainly ecclesiastical, of course, and lives and thrives in safe contentment, not with this world to be sure, but with another one which by all accounts is greatly more unequal or undivine and vicious even than this. It comprises all of every sect who regard the traditional church as directly in the line of man's spiritual welfare, or as supplying by Divine appointment a literal pathway to heaven.' [16]

Of these two classes, the former is really parasitic upon the latter. Moralism must be allowed a comparatively recent disease. The Church 'historically breeds, sweats, or throws off from its flanks, the civilized state of man [James uses the word *civilized* in the contemptuous sense of Fourier, much as the Marxians use *bourgeois*], and morality is the unquestionable law of civilization, the absolute substance, condition, and measure of all our civic righteousness.' 'Vast numbers of persons, indeed, are to be found in every community, who—having as yet attained to no spiritual insight or understanding—are entirely content with, nay, proud of, the moral "purple and fine linen" with which they are daily decked out in the favorable esteem of their friends, and are meanwhile at hearty peace with themselves.' [17] Unitarianism is the movement which best represents moralism: it takes moral character and 'good works' as absolute, and as making men righteous in the sight of God. But Unitarianism still preserves the semblance of a church, though the disguise be more or less transparent. Outside the 'churches' entirely, moralism can and does flourish—as Transcendentalism, as 'ethical culture,' as philanthropy. The New England conscience, with its fussy self-consciousness and self-culture, seldom transcends moralism.

The church, however, is the more flagrant offender. Religion was intended to wean man not merely from the 'world' but from himself and his personal pretensions to righteousness; not to assure man of finding personal favor in the sight of God, but to promise redemption from all personal hopes and fears through incorporation in the mystical Body of Christ, solidarity, in other words, with all his kind. 'Religion was once a spiritual life in the earth, though a very rude and terrible one . . . Then she meant terror and amazement to all devout self-complacency in man; then she meant rebuke and denial to every form of distinctively *personal* hope and pretension towards God; then she meant discredit and death to every breath of a pharisaic or quaker temper in humanity, by which a man could be led to boast of a "private spirit" in his bosom, giving him a differential character and aspect in God's sight to other men. . . .'[18]

Conscience, the organ through which our spiritual life begins to operate, was never intended to make us self-complacent, thanking God that we are not as our sinful fellows. Like the Law, its office was meant to be purely negative: to convict us of sin. James follows St Paul in his indictment of legalism. All men have come short of the Law. But then the Law intended death, not life: it showed us the corruption of Adam and all his spiritual progeny in order that, turning away from personal and moral hopes, we should turn our hearts towards the Gospel and its promise of life to those who love the brethren.

Alas, the church, the representative or formal church, has often fallen into the legalism it arose to confound. It has assured men of absolute difference between saint and sinner, and given them hope of finding personal favor in God's sight.

Three sorts of religious experience are equally offensive to James: the Unitarian variety, which thinks of God primarily as a Divine Moral Being, who is gratified by our personal advances in ethical culture;

the Catholic variety, whether Roman or Anglican,
which considers right relations between God and man
as essentially *ex opere operato,* ceremonially or ritually
achieved; the Evangelical variety, which takes an erotic
or at any rate sentimental turn, and dispenses with
moral and ceremonial relations only in order to substitute a purely *personal* intimacy. James illustrates
this third variety, still not extinct, by recalling an acquaintance of his, a loquacious person who said, 'I
can't imagine how any one should have any distrust
of God. For my part, if I were once in His presence,
I should feel like *cuddling-up* to Him as instinctively
as I would cuddle-up to the sunshine or fire in a
wintry day.' James adds, 'It is beautiful to observe
how utterly destitute Swedenborg found the angelic
mind of all this putrid sentimentality, this abject *personal* piety.' [19]

Though a fourth sort of religious experience with
which he was familiar, the Calvinistic, was also offensive to James, he preferred it to the other three,
on the ground of its virile contempt for moralism
and sentimentality, its sense of the gulf between Creator and creature.

V

Only the shallow, whether within or without the
church, can rest in moralism. The Law is our school-
master to bring us to Christ: those who most assiduously attempt to obey the Law will soonest confess
their complete insufficiency for their task, will soonest

surrender to the Gospel. Conscience similarly arrests our spiritual development at moralism only when we grow slothful, inattentive; when we pause at partial or purely ceremonial compliance with her precepts.

'It is very true that conscience is the sole arbiter of good and evil to man; and that persons of a literal and superficial turn of mind . . . may easily fancy themselves in spiritual harmony with it, or persuade themselves and others that they have fully satisfied every claim of its righteousness. But minds of a deeper quality soon begin to suspect that the demands of conscience are not so easily satisfied, soon discover in fact that it is a ministration of death exclusively, and not of life, to which they are abandoning themselves. For what conscience inevitably teaches its earnest votaries ere long is, to give up the hopeless efforts to reconcile good and evil in their practise, and learn to identify themselves, on the contrary, with the evil principle alone, while they assign all good exclusively to God.' [20]

The revelation of God in Jesus Christ offers the way out of legalism, and turns us from our self-righteousness and Pharisaism to a life beyond good and evil, a life of love and spontaneous brotherhood: The New Testament 'addresses no inviting or soothing word of any sort to the saint, but only to the sinner. In one of these very rare gospel incidents which give us a glimpse into Christ's *personal* temperament, a saintly youth presents himself so aglow with all moral excellence, that Christ cannot help testifying a natural

impulse of affection towards him; but he nevertheless straightway charges him to set no value upon his
virtue as a *celestial* qualification. "If thou wilt be
perfect, go and *sell all that thou hast. . . ."* [21]

The way out of legalism is first of all negative: to
cease piquing ourselves upon our distinctions from
others, our possessions, our virtues. How hardly shall
the *rich man,* the man of parts, powers, personal pretensions, enter into the Kingdom of Heaven! Progress,
indeed, 'whether public or private, seems to take
place in an invariably negative way, that is, it always
exacts a preliminary experience and acknowledgement
of evil and error. Our vices and follies, collective and
personal, have wrought us infinitely more advantage
than our virtue and knowledge have ever achieved.
Our best learning has come to us in the way of un-
learning our prejudice, our best wisdom in the way
of outgrowing conceit. . . . So palpably true is all
this, that the fundamental grace of the religious character throughout history is humility; the primary evidence of a spiritual quickening in the soul, re-
pentance.' [22]

At the time of Christ's advent, 'the stoics were the
leaders of speculative thought. To fall back on all
occasions upon one's moral force, and find a refuge
against calamity in one's native strength of will, was
the best recognized wisdom of man. . . . Christ probably had never heard of the stoics, but if he had he
could only have been revolted by their doctrine, since
his own was the exact and total inversion of theirs.

The ideal of the stoic was rich and cultivated manhood. The ideal of Christ was innocent unconscious childhood. According to Christ, what men need in order to the full enjoyment of the divine favor is, to be emptied of all personal pretension, to become indifferent to all self-seeking or self-providence. . . .' [23]

The message of Christianity has been sadly misinterpreted by the Church. The 'doctrine of the Christ is nothing more and nothing less than a revelation of the *essential* unity of God and man. . . . No matter what the occasion may have been, you find him invariably identifying himself with the interests of the most enlarged humanity, and ready to sacrifice every private tie which in any way involved a denial of the universal brotherhood of the race.' [24] But the orthodox church has substituted for Jesus' zeal for humanity, a 'zeal for the person of Jesus himself.' The church 'makes Jesus under the name of a mediator, a perpetual barrier to the cordial intercourse of God and man.' According to its teaching, Jesus 'exhausts the worth of human nature, so that no man created by God can ever appear tolerable to God, unless shining with his reflected lustre.' He converts Jesus into 'a monster of self-seeking,' and turns 'the grace of the gospel into a mere argument of his personal supremacy.' We believe in his personal pretensions, or we are damned. He is indeed alleged as having done us a signal favor (dying to reconcile us to an angry God); but he then claims our worship in return, 'under penalty of death, under penalty of everlasting misery.

It is a purely diabolic claim, which all humanity disowns with loathing and contempt.'

The Lord is Swedenborg's name for the God-Man,
God Incarnate. James refuses to identify the God-Man
with the historic Jesus, but interprets the term as de-
noting the union of God with man. 'By the Lord
regarded spiritually or rationally, then, we do not
mean any literal or personal man, capable of being
sensibly comprehended; but we mean that Divine
and universal life in man, which grows out of the
conjunction of the infinite Divine Love with our
finite natural love . . .' [25]

VI

What state, now, are we to look to as fulfilling the
destiny of mankind? Moralism we know; *civilization,*
its social equivalent, we know. The Law we know;
but what then is the Gospel? How shall we conceive
of the final union between God and man?

To none of these questions does Mr James afford
us precise answers. Man's final state is nowhere open
to scientific observation. Creation implies Redemption: James 'scorned to admit, even as a possibility,
that the great and loving Creator, who has all the
being and the power, and has brought us as far as *this,*
should not bring us *through,* and *out,* into the most
triumphant harmony.' [26] But only revelation can give
us belief in such a harmony; and revelation never
discloses *facts* but only truths.

The state *beyond* moralism is spiritual Christianity; the state *beyond* 'civilization' is socialism, or, since *socialism* has come to mean a special sort of organization, we had better say Society. James does not look forward to the substitution for the existing governments of some other sort of government, but to the abolition of all government. In other words, he is a philosophic anarchist. Governments belong to the dispensation of the Law; with the full advent of the Gospel, they will pass away. James would say with St Augustine, *Ama et fac quod vis.*

The State will cease; so will the Church. Its sovereignty too is provisional and vicarious. When God's living presence in Society comes to be recognized, no representative ritual will be necessary. God will no longer be thought of as dwelling in temples made by hands; his glory will be made manifest in his tabernacling among men.

Men will have passed beyond the moral life, with its good and evil. Heaven and hell, 'both alike nothing but logical, ordinary, and inevitable spiritual incidents of our *natural* or race evolution,' will both finally 'coalesce in that final unitary display of omnipotent goodness and wisdom known as human SOCIETY, or the Lord's KINGDOM UPON EARTH.' [27]

The distinctive character of the moral life is choice; its distinctive operation is obedience to *duty*. 'The element of will or choice is everything in the moral life, and the fussy votaries of it accordingly are absurdly tenacious of their personal merit. But this ele-

ment of will or choice scarcely enters appreciably into
the spiritual life, unless into the lowest forms of it;
and in all the higher or celestial forms it is unknown.'[28]
Choice will pass away in favor of spontaneity. We
shall *love and do what we will.*

In some such *myth* would James deliver to us the
New Jerusalem as it will *appear;* the *reality,* the essence of this consummation, will consist in the union
of God with his creatures.

VII

And now we must ask what James means by God.
As William has said of his father, he 'nowhere attempts by metaphysical or empirical arguments to
make the existence of God plausible; he simply assumes it . . .', or, as Miss Kellogg puts it, 'Mr James
looks at creation instinctively from the creative side
. . . The usual problem is,—given the creation, to
find the creator. To Mr James it is,—given the creator,
to find the creation. God is; of His being there is no
doubt; but who and what are *we?'*[29]

William James appears to have believed his father
a theist, for all he admits that 'common-sense theism,
the popular religion of our European race, has, through
all its apparent variations, remained essentially faithful to pluralism,' while his father was an uncompro-
mising monist.[30] Theism, however,—or deism, as the
elder James prefers to call it—holds to a belief in a
God in some sense personal—either, as in Nicene

Christianity, to the view that personality exists in God, or, with the older Unitarianism, to the view that God *is* a Person.[81]

But James sharply rebukes all belief in a personal God, a God external to his creatures. God is not outside us, another if greater self. He is not a self, not a person at all. The self is the badge and limitation of mankind.

James adduces Swedenborg's description of the angels as 'never thinking of the Lord from person, "because thought determined to person limits and degrades the truth. . . ."; . . . the angels are amazed at the stupidity of church people "in not suffering themselves to be elevated out of the letter of the revelation, and persisting to think carnally, and not spiritually of the Lord,—as of his flesh and blood, and not of his infinite goodness and truth." '

To 'be a conscious person is to be *self*-centred, and to be God is to be not only without self-hood, but identical with universal life or being. . . .' Spiritual nearness to God 'implies infinite personal remoteness from him, since God avouches himself to be universal life or being, which is flagrantly incompatible either with the fact or the sentiment of personality.'

James denies that God is 'a person finited from man by space and time,' and affirms that God is 'the inmost and inseparable life of every man great or small, wise or stupid, good or evil.' Even the literal Christian verity, he thinks, 'justifies us in ascribing to Him henceforth a distinctly NATURAL or impersonal in-

finitude, and so forever rids us both of the baleful
intellectual falsities inherent in the conception of His
supernatural personality, and of the enforced personal
homage, precatory and deprecatory, engendered by
that conception in the sphere of our sentimental piety.'
He avows, 'I have not the least sentiment of worship
for His name, the least sentiment of awe or reverence
towards Him, considered as a perfect person sufficient
unto Himself. That style of deity exerts no attraction either upon my heart or understanding. Any
mother who suckles her babe upon her own breast, any
bitch in fact who litters her periodical brood of pups,
presents to my imagination a vastly nearer and sweeter
Divine charm.' [32]

Who or what then is God? Swedenborg tells us
that 'God is very man.' [33] This has often been translated, conformably to the presupposition of orthodox
theism, into 'God is a *man*'; and the orthodox New
Churchmen have made of it that Jesus, or the Lord, is
alone God. James takes Swedenborg as meaning that
God is not *a man*, but MAN. 'DEISM as a philosophic
doctrine, that is, as importing an essential difference
between the divine and human natures, or God and
man, is a philosophic absurdity. There is no God but
the Lord, or our glorified NATURAL humanity, and
whatsoever other deity we worship is but a baleful
idol of our own spiritual fantasy, whom we supersti-
tiously project into nature to scourge us into *quasi*
or provisional manhood, while as yet we are blind to
the spiritual truth.' [34]

Heaven is heaven because the persons who compose it 'are used to acknowledge God only *in natural or associated form,* and not in any ideal spiritual or personal form which they might sensuously think more consonant with his perfection. . . .'

'In short, my reader, if human nature, the human race, mankind, or humanity, be not *spiritually* the only true name of God, exhausting the conception, then I at least do not know the true name of God, and certainly should never care to know it.'[35]

Does this mean that God is merely universal man, a kind of Platonic *idea* in which all men participate, by participation in which they become men? Or is James, like Comte, urging the substitution of Humanity for God as the object of our worship? This is the most obscure point in James' thought. He expressly dissociates himself from Comte's doctrine;[36] and he would require some more dynamic relationship of creator to created than that of *idea* to particulars. Yet reject the ordinary theistic view, the Platonic, the Comtean, and what fourth view remains? God is affirmed Universal Man, the sole spiritual meaning and unity of the race; are we to understand that he (to use the personal pronoun as James does, for purposes of convenience) is more than this? Is he merely immanent in man, or does he transcend the utmost reach of our associated spiritual potencies?

The impression remains that James is sincere in rejecting the Comtean view of God as inadequate. God is more than the sum total of men, not in the least an abstraction, a generalization, an idea; all of these conceptions are too inert. James conceives of God as active, as indeed the *one really active* force in the universe, the one true substance. We do not make God in our image; but, in some deep if obscure sense, he makes us in his. It is as intolerable to James as to any Augustinian to believe that men's ordinary selves can effect any great work. The old theology gone, the problem of grace is still left. What have we which is not given us? It was a germinal conviction with James that 'the individual man, as such, is nothing, but owes all he is and has to the race nature he inherits, and to the society in which he was born.'[87] But how can there be more in the race nature, as such, than the sum total of our individual natures? The old dispute between Realist, Conceptualist, and Nominalist.

Mr James tells us that 'the race alone is *real* man, and invariably sets the tune, therefore, for us paltry, personal or phenomenal men to march to. And consequently we turn out good or evil persons—that is to say, even *phenomenally* good or evil men—just as we consent or refuse to keep step with the race's music.'[88] But who sets the tune? And the *real man* is of course not the sum total of men, or an average of all men, but the spiritual meaning of man,—what he may be when Redemption has completed its work and the kingdoms of this world have become the kingdoms of our God, and man has assumed his redeemed form in Society. The *Real Man* is a sort of Aristotelian *final cause*: the point of life, of history, is its *End*.

If we ask James whether Man exhausts the meaning
of God, he will perhaps tell us that God *in himself* is
Infinite Love and Infinite Wisdom. Further, 'He of
all beings is the *least* free, has the *least* power, to act
arbitrarily, or follow his own caprice. . . .'[39] But God
in himself we cannot know: we can know only the
Lord, the God-Man, or 'the infinite Divine love and
wisdom in union with every soul of man.'

In short, James denies a personal God outside of
humanity, to regard God as the creative principle
within humanity. We might call this principle the
Life-Force, were it not that such an affiliation would
do an injustice to James' insistence upon Man as the
exclusive meaning of nature, and Society as the exclusive meaning of man.

Can such a world view be called Christian? William
James quite rightly confesses inability 'to see any radical and essential necessity for the mission of Christ in
his [father's] scheme of the universe. A "fall" there
is, and a redemption; but . . . I cannot help thinking
that if my father had been born outside the pale of
Christendom, he might perfectly well have brought
together all the other elements of his system, much
as it stands now. . . .'[40]

I quite subscribe to this judgment; indeed, I think
Mr James' doctrine must have struck the ordinary
church-goer, had he understood it, as atheism. Even
William overmuch applies the word *theologian* to his
father. The 'theology' is largely a matter of terminology.[41] James was trained as a theologian, and his early

reading in Swedenborg supplied him with a vocabulary which he became dexterous in turning to his own purpose. But this terminology, to which James assigned a purely 'humanitary' meaning, was inevitably taken by his readers, alike those professional at religion and those outside it, in approximately their customary theological sense. This made for confusion and misunderstanding, a misunderstanding which a certain perverse side of James apparently relished, and which he certainly made little effort to clear up.

But as James' God is something more than Comte's, so his philosophy transcends the sort of positivistic socialism he found about him. Towards the end of his life he confesses himself not the least indisposed to believe himself destined by the Divine providence—'either in my own person or the persons of my descendants—to the possible enjoyment of health, wealth, and all manner of outward prosperity, in the evolution of a final natural order for man on the earth, or the development of a united race-personality.' [42] But this is not enough. When he is invited to regard the *natural destiny* of the race as adequate satisfaction to men's faith, he pronounces it 'inexpressibly revolting. For after all is said that can be said, it is a mere reduction to order of man's natural or constitutional life, with the spiritual, functional, or infinite side of his being left out. And are men content to deem themselves cattle, that they expect no higher boon at the hands of the DIVINE NATURAL HUMANITY but an unexampled provision for their board and lodging?'

It is the spirit that quickeneth. What is needed is not so much some further legislation, some reordering of our government or even our economic system. Given the social spirit, these changes will come of themselves. But the essence of the matter is not in them. The essence of the matter is the full consciousness on my part that *vir* is nothing apart from *homo;* that I live only in my race; and the consequent will to surrender myself to my fellows, and lose myself in the Lord, that is, in Society. Any other than a *religious* way of putting this seems to James to fall short of expressing his conviction that the whole process is not external but of the heart.

Mr James' uniqueness as a thinker lies precisely in this identification of the spiritual and the social, not to the extinction of either the spiritual or the social, but to the enrichment of both.

EPILOGUE

MEN may serve their times—and posterity—in a variety of ways: some by performance, others by contemplation; some by holding up to scorn the superficial standards of their day and the false hopes, others by announcing the gospel. Some prophets cry in the wilderness, others command urban pulpits; some found sects and parties committed to perpetuating their temperamental idiom equally with their insight; others—and these perhaps not the least fortunate—leave no establishment to wrangle scholastically over the master's *ipsissima verba.*

James, says Santayana, was 'one of those somewhat obscure sages whom early America produced: mystics of independent mind, hermits in the desert of business, and heretics in the churches.' He stood aloof, assuredly, from those who thought the kingdom of God came with observation. Paradoxical in so many respects, he preached a social gospel without commit-

ting himself to any political or ecclesiastical organization; and his severest criticism befell those who thought
to further by 'practical' plans and projects that redemption of man in the imminence of which he believed with optimistic determinism. The world was
not to be saved by Brook Farm nor yet by the 'soi-
disant New Jerusalem.'

This detachment, so alien to the expansiveness of
his personality, proceeded in part from his genial distrust of cranks and freaks, in part from his sense of
humor, in part, again, from his common sense.

Doubtless he was troubled at times by the possession of economic security and leisure unshared by most
of his fellows; but, generous as he proved with individuals, he never surrendered his fortune. A wealthy
socialist who joined no party and trusted to his books
to make his contribution to the new order: how could
he hope to escape satire and rebuke from those who
entrusted their all to communistic experiment and
were willing to risk reputation and life for their
cause? William Lloyd Garrison, George Ripley,
Stephen Pearl Andrews, Bronson Alcott: these are all
figures with something of the heroic in them. Andrews
satirized James as a 'parlor Socialist.' All the brave
and humorless reformers of the day would have felt
some doubt of a rich man's entry into the Kingdom
of Heaven.

In our own day we have heard the Socialist candidate
for the Presidency pour scorn on the liberals of *The
New Republic;* and the orthodox Communists (the

few who enjoy the purity of a scholastic Marxism) ex-communicate the literary gentlemen who, though cognizant of their *bourgeois* breeding and the evils of any save a *proletarian* gospel, still possess too much refinement and imagination to use the new terminology without an accent. With these gentry James would belong today, and with them he would be damned— as theoretical and critical, not turning his hand to getting votes and passing bills and drawing members to the meetings of the 'local' and organizing strikes. His was a religion of the study, not the market-place.

Though his offense could be palliated, such indictment must remain, on its own ground, largely unanswerable. But the blow may be parried. Is it by any means so certain that a direct offensive is the only way of making war on the enemy? Are Fabian tactics to be totally discredited? May not a sinuous propaganda prove at least as effective as that which is openly belligerent? James possessed a serene confidence that truth is great and will prevail: not in his time, not even in his children's or grandchildren's times, perhaps. No man knows, he would feel, the day or the hour when God shall be incarnated in the social order. We must not be in haste, though we must not cease to hope. And our hope must be in educating men's imaginations and consciences. The machinery of organization and legislation: what can that avail? Laws passed in advance of men's conversion to new standards are premature and can never be enforced; and after men's conversion they will be unnecessary.

James' refusal to coöperate with agencies which would appear to have been working for the ends dear to him often seems ungracious and pedantic. In his favorite journalistic bouts with the reformers and philanthropists of his day, he frequently seems insistent on principles rather than expedients and, what is more irritating, on terminology rather than principles. Yet the impression does injustice. James really judged that the busy idealists all about him were at work without having *thought* enough, that they were too impatient to *do* to achieve that far-sighted and catholic view of human needs without which all their efforts would effect only meager good or positive damage. Against the Fourierists he urged that they were attempting to make outward organization accomplish the work reserved for regeneration. And against Garrison and his allies of the *Liberator,* that they were tinkering with details of the social order when what was required was a complete change of motivation and a whole new philosophy of life: 'if all these specific reforms of yours claimed the authentication of some more universal doctrine than they themselves constitute, or were themselves housed in some more general truth as wide as human hope, and therefore able to enlist *every* interest in its behalf, they would be greatly enhanced in importance to the popular conscience.'

When men are ready for it, and the new order comes, it will be a *totum simul*. As specific reforms, by arresting social disease, delay the death of the moribund world, so an individual's anticipations of the new world are ineffectual, albeit dramatic, gestures. What effect upon the masses could Brook Farm or Fruitlands or any of the other little groups of the high-minded experimentalists exert? Suppose James had allowed his expansive sentiments to master him and had flung his wealth to the popular winds? Of course the very melodrama of the thing, the attention (albeit favorable) it would have called to him as an individual, would have been offensive to his taste as well as to his deep conviction, which he shared with our present-day Communists, that not philanthropy —the rich giving to the poor—was needed, but social justice, the economic equalization of the community. Though he would have violently dissented from their doctrine of a proletarian Revolution, he would have agreed, heartily, that private philanthropy is an abomination: like specific reform, it patches the old vesture instead of providing the imperatively needed new.

Clearly James would have no sympathy with Marxian materialism and the strictly economic basis of its social doctrine. For him, ethics—or rather, as he would have said, Christianity—must precede economics. Men's hearts must be transformed before their *mores*.

His religion was perhaps *sui generis*. He could not abide Calvinism, nor High Church ritualism, nor Evangelical preoccupation with one's own spiritual temperature, nor the unlicensed emotions of the revivalist, nor the Unitarian's complacence over his moral character and public benevolence. Yet he cannot be reduced to the dimensions of a complete secularist.

He would have understood the religion of Sovietism, with its almost mystical devotion to the state, yet he would have judged that not enough. His objections to the naturalism of Fourier and Comte would have held also against Marx.

Was it respect for tradition and the desire for continuity which kept him to the terminology of religion? Scarcely. He showed no filial reverence for the Calvinistic theology of his father. He was no Biblicist and no Sabbatarian. He was a dissident from the conventional views of marriage and the family. Not the old Christianity but the new, the coming Church of God among men, stirred his heart and his imagination.

No current sect or 'ethical culture society' or 'community church' would have satisfied him. To substitute the lecture or the forum for worship of an anthropomorphic Monarch in the skies is but dubious gain. Though our virtue needs to be informed and thoughtful, religion cannot equate adult education.

Religion is not 'morality touched with emotion' but morality transcended, transmuted into love. All ethical legalism and all scrupulosity of conscience will yield to the supremacy of *charitas*. Love is the fulfilment of the Law.

It would be easy to convict James' ardorous pages of antinomianism. Like Carlyle and Emerson, he was deeply shocked by the Victorian substitution of respectability for virtue, of *moralism* for spirituality. But his life defends the purity of his motives. He sought for himself no relaxation of nineteenth cen-

tury ethics and lived within the letter of the Law
while he condemned its *spirit* as ready to be superseded by the Gospel.

The Law prescribes long catalogues of injunctions
and taboos; the Gospel trusts to the enunciation of a
few spiritual principles which the faithful will apply
to every particular case of conscience they encounter.
James offers no code of right living, private or social.
He is concerned to convert his readers to a way of
thinking and feeling about life, to a vision of what life
might (and shall) be. He is as impatient of ecclesiastical as of political machinery. Why this etiquette of
virtue? *Love God and do what you will.*

This is all mysticism, some will say. It makes no
provision for the masses of men who live not by first-
hand experience of religion but, derivatively, by the
insight of the prophets and saints. If 'organized religion' descends to the perceptions of the majority, it
elevates the perceptions of the majority above their
'natural' level; if it 'accommodates,' it also preserves.
Most men need rules and prescriptions and *mores;*
and the Church does wisely by compromising between
the Law and the Gospel.

Would James have dissented from all this? In writing, probably, but not in practise; for he was as distinguished for common sense as for speculative nicety.
His business as a writer, he would have felt, was not
with expediency. Other men might be called to op-
portunism, not he. His favoring circumstances of economic and intellectual detachment made it his duty

to speak the *final truth* as he saw it, without adaptation to individual cases or regard to practical consequences. He that hath ears to hear, let him hear.

Too averse to autobiography to enter upon any *apologia* for himself and his methods, James undoubtedly felt a strong sense of vocation. 'His truths were his life.' He was to sow in faith: God would give the harvest in His own time.

James' contribution to American thought was not a program but a vision. Men need both; but programs and their constructors pass away when they have made their contribution to the emergencies of the hour. Because they read not the times but the eternities, the men of vision belong to the permanent treasure of mankind. James' life movingly illustrates the heroism possible to the intellectual who steadfastly bears his witness whether the world heeds or not. His vision of Society as the Redeemed Form of Man takes its place with those American apocalypses which stimulate the imagination and stir the faith.

NOTES

CHAPTER I

1. Hastings, *William James of Albany* (1924), 3.
2. Manning, James H., *New York State Men* (1911–22), no. 116, 'William James.' *Cf.* Larrabee, *The American Scholar,* I, 402.
3. Hastings, *William James,* 1–2.
4. Larrabee, 'Henry James, Sr. '30 at Union,' *Union Alumni Monthly,* XV, 239.
5. Grattan, *The Three Jameses,* 20.
6. *Last Will and Testament of William James, Esq. of the City of Albany* (There is a copy in the Boston Public Library). *Cf.* also *American Biographical Dictionary,* ed. Wm. Allen (Boston, 3rd edition, 1857), under 'William James.'
7. Hastings, *William James,* 4–5.
8. *Ibid.,* 5–6.
9. *Literary Remains of Henry James,* ed. William James (1884), 147–9. *Letters of William James* (1920), I, 5–6. *Literary Remains* furnishes a quotation from 'Immortal Life: Illustrated in a Brief Autobiographical Sketch of the late Stephen Dewhurst, Edited, with an Introduction, by Henry James.' According to William James, (*Re-*

mains, 7) Stephen Dewhurst is an 'entirely fictitious personage,' and the autobiography is his father's own. The elder Henry James 'had often been urged by members of his family to express his religious philosophy under the form of a personal evolution of opinion. But egotistic analysis was less to his taste than enunciation of objective results; so that, although he sat down to the autobiographic task a good many times, it was at long intervals'; and *Society the Redeemed Form of Man* (1879) was written after the Autobiography was begun.

James took such slight interest in the 'facts' of his own (or another's) life that little in the way of chronicle is vouchsafed. Even the development of his 'inner life,' a theme of greater interest to him, is, without much doubt, interpreted in the light of his mature philosophy, and is, to that extent, to be read with caution. But in lieu of more objective witness, his biographer has seen best to introduce here, and subsequently in this chapter, James' recollections of his early feelings and attitudes.

10. *Literary Remains*, 149–51. The grandmother described was his mother's mother.
11. *Ibid.*, 152.
12. *Ibid.*, 153.
13. *Literature and Dogma* (Boston, 1873), 53.
14. *Literary Remains*, 158.
15. *Ibid.*, 159.
16. *Ibid.*, 154.
17. *Ibid.*, 172.
18. *Ibid.*, 187–9.
19. *Ibid.*, 162–3; 189–91.
20. *Ibid.*, 183.
21. *Letters of William James*, I, 7–8. The professor who directed the experiments in balloon-flying is here said to have been Joseph Henry, later head of the Smithsonian Institution, but Dr Larrabee (*Union Alumni Monthly*,

XV, 242), points out that Professor Henry did not take up his duties at the Academy until Sept. 1826, while the accident occurred not later than the summer of 1824. Henry James (II) in *Notes of a Son and Brother* (1914), speaks of his father as so lamed for life 'that he could circulate to any convenience but on even surfaces and was indeed mainly reduced to driving—it had made him for all his earlier time an excellent whip'(192).

In *Early Years of the Saturday Club* (1918), 327, E. W. Emerson says Mr James 'limped along on his wooden leg with some agility. . . .'

22. Obituary of Mr James in Boston *Daily Advertiser*, Dec. 20, 1882, and 'Henry James, Sr.' (an interview), Boston *Sunday Herald*, April 17, 1881.

23. See *Memoirs of Eliphalet Nott, D.D., L.L.D.* by C. Van Santvoord (N.Y., 1876).

24. *Memoirs*, 57–9, 64–5.

25. The financial relationship between Nott and James is the discovery of Codman Hislop, a member of the Department of English at Union College. For a full account of the transactions, *cf.* 'James Symposium,' Schenectady, N. Y., *Gazette*, Jan. 23, 1933. For an abridged account, *cf.* Larrabee, *The American Scholar*, I, 408.

26. Sanborn, E. B., 'The Opinions of the late Dr Nott,' *Atlantic Monthly*, XX (1877), 527–32.

27. For the Union curriculum of the time in more detail, see *Historical Sketch of Union College* (Washington, 1876), 26–31.

28. 'Henry James, Sr. '30, at Union,' by Harold A. Larrabee, *Union Alumni Monthly*, XV (May 1926), 242–3.

29. An account of his class in 'Kames' is given in the *Memoirs*, 132–3.

30. *Memoirs*, 174–5.

31. 'Locke's mind,' writes Emerson's friend, Sampson Reed, 'will not always be the standard of metaphysics. Had

we a description of it in its present state, it would make a very different book from "Locke on the Human Understanding".' ('Genius', in *Aesthetic Papers* [1849], 63.)

32. *Memoirs*, 282–9.

33. *Memoirs*, 226–7.

34. Larrabee, *Union Alumni Monthly*, XV, 243; Grattan, *The Three Jameses*, 28. According to Hislop, James likely holds the dubious honor of being the first man in America to wear a fraternity 'badge.'

35. The younger James writes: 'My father, when considerably past his thirtieth year, if I am not mistaken, had travelled "East," within our borders, but once in his life— on the occasion of his spending two or three months in Boston as a very young man. . . .' (*Notes*, 188.)

    The Boston sojourn was the consequence of a 'misunderstanding, if indeed not of a sharp rupture, for the time, with a highly generous but also on occasion strongly protesting parent at Albany, a parent displeased with some course he had taken or had declined to take (there was a tradition among us that he had been for a period quite definitely "wild"). . . .' (*Ibid.*, 189.)

36. McIntyre's letter and James', hitherto unpublished, are drawn from *Concerning William James of Albany* in the Theatre Collection of the Widener Library.

37. Isaac Jackson, tutor at Union from 1826, Professor of Mathematics from 1831–   , was the author of *Elements of Comic Sections* (1854), *Elementary Treatise on Optics* (1854), *Elementary Treatise on Mechanics*. (*Historical Sketch of Union College*, 17, 20, 25.) The letter addressed to Jackson, the earliest of James which is known to survive, has never before been published; it comes from the Widener collection of James papers.

38. Francis Jenks edited the *Christian Examiner,* the Unitarian review of Boston, from 1826 to 1831 (*cf.* W. Cushing's *Index.* . . . , Boston, 1879. Preface).

39. The Rev. William Ellery Channing (d. 1842) served but one parish, the Federal St. Church, Boston.
40. The Rev. Alonzo Potter was rector of St Paul's Church, Boston, from 1826 to 1832. He had married, in 1824, the only daughter of President Nott. Likely James had met the Potters in Schenectady.
41. *Letters of William James, I.* 'At this time, he was much in the company of the son of Gov. De Witt Clinton. . . .' (Boston *Sunday Herald,* 17 April, 1881).
42. The *Craftsman* was published at Rochester by E. J. Roberts, and removed to Albany some time in the latter part of 1831. The issue of Oct. 29, 1831, bears the names of Roberts, I. T. Simmons, and H. James; Simmons dropped out Nov. 12 of that year. James' name appears through the issue of Feb. 6, 1832. The paper, a four-page affair, devoted three pages to advertising and the fourth to the proceedings of the legislature and Congress, a few items of general news, and editorial battles with the Albany *Argus.*

I owe my information concerning the *Craftsman* to Joseph Gavit, Esq., Senior Librarian of the New York State Library at Albany.

CHAPTER II

1. Rev. William James (1797–1858) retired from the pastorate twenty-three years before his death to devote his time to philosophical and theological research. Under the title, *Grace for Grace,* he published a volume of theological letters. 'His mind was generally teeming with profound thought, and was never in its element while moving in a beaten track. His taste in composition was so remark-

ably exact as to set at defiance the sternest criticism. His discourses for the pulpit were generally elaborated with the utmost care, and it must be acknowledged were better fitted to furnish material for thought to thoroughly disciplined minds, than to minister to the gratification of the superficial and emotional hearer. . . .' *(An Address Delivered on Occasion of the Funeral of the Rev. William James, D.D.* By William B. Sprague, D.D., [Albany, 1868], 18.) Dr Sprague further describes Dr James as 'somewhat morbid,' speaks of his enthusiasm and impulsiveness, and remarks: 'his peculiarities of temperament were not in harmony with the uniform routine of pastoral life.' (p. 19). For the facts of his life, *cf.* Mrs Katherine Hastings' *William James of Albany* . . . (1924), 8–9.

2. *General Catalogue of the Theological Seminary, Princeton, New Jersey, from 1812—1856,* under 1835—6.

3. 'Henry James, Sr.,' (a report of an interview), Boston *Sunday Herald,* April 17, 1881.

4. *Literary Remains,* 124.

5. *The Nature of Evil* (N. Y., 1855), 124, 126. Dr Samuel Miller (1769–1850), Professor of Ecclesiastical History at the Seminary from 1813, was celebrated for his character as 'Christian gentleman' and wrote a book which went into three editions, *Letters on Clerical Manners and Habits: Addressed to a Student in the Theological Seminary, at Princeton, N. J.* (1827).

6. *Literary Remains,* 138.

7. *Ibid.,* 125–6.

8. *Ibid.,* 128.

9. *Ibid.,* 130.

10. For an extended account of the 'years of strife,' see Gillett, *History of the Presbyterian Church in the United States* (Philadelphia, 1864), II, 456–502.

11. *A Letter of the Rev. Samuel Miller, D.D., Professor in the Theological Seminary at Princeton, New Jersey; Ad-*

*dressed to the Members of the Presbyterian Churches in
the United States on the Present Crisis in Their Religious
and Theological Concerns* (Hartford [Conn.], 1833).

12. On the Exscinding Acts see R. E. Thompson, *History
    of the Presbyterian Churches* (N. Y., 1895); for the found-
    ing of Union, *ibid.*, 113–4.

13. *The Nature of Evil*, 250, 254.

14. *Ibid.*, 254–5, 256–9.

15. Obituary of Mr James in the *Boston Daily Advertiser*,
    Dec. 20, 1882.

16. Joseph Henry served for two years as tutor in the family
    of Stephen van Rensselaer; in 1826, he became Profes-
    sor of Mathematical and Natural Philosophy at Albany
    Academy; in 1832, he was elected Professor of Natural
    Philosophy at Princeton (the 'College of New Jersey');
    and in 1846, he became first director of the Smithsonian
    Institute. (*D. A. B.,* VIII, 550–3).

    The unpublished correspondence between Joseph Henry
    and Henry James is preserved in the library of the Smith-
    sonian Institute at Washington.

17. In 1837, Princeton had given Joseph Henry a year's leave
    of absence for study abroad. His friend Dr A. Dallas
    Bache, Benjamin Franklin's great-grandson, served, from
    1828, as Professor of Natural Philosophy in the Univer-
    sity of Pennsylvania; in 1836, he was sent abroad for two
    years to study European methods of education (*D. A. B.,* I,
    461–2).

18. The letter is dated June 15, 1837.

19. *Notes,* 266–7. The novelist confessedly draws upon his
    imagination as well as his memory of his father's anecdotes
    for his version of the Irish visit. Mr Henry James has
    written me that what he saw on a visit to Bailieborough
    in 1931 persuades him that his uncle romanticized the
    story which, as a child, he heard from his father. Bailie-
    borough, a hundred years ago, must have been an agri-

cultural community around a small market village, where there could hardly have been a 'professional class.' The farmers under the Irish land system would have been tenants, and the dwellings which his grandfather might have visited in 1837 would have been very modest. But there seem to him to be numerous indications that the family were careful and self-regarding folk who managed to give their children the equivalent of a good school education.

20. Robert Sandeman (1718–71), born in Scotland, educated at St Andrews, linen manufacturer and then preacher, came to America in 1764, and established societies of his faith in Boston (see 'The Places of Worship of the Sandemanians in Boston,' Publications of the Colonial Society of Mass., VI, 109–23) and other places in New England. His gravestone, in the burying-ground at Danbury, Conn., bears the following vigorous inscription: 'Here lies, until the resurrection, the body of ROBERT SANDEMAN, a native of Perth, North Britain, who, in the face of continual opposition from all sorts of men, long boldly contended for the ancient faith, that the bare word of Jesus Christ, without a deed or thought on the part of man, is sufficient to present the chief of sinners spotless before God. To declare this blessed truth, as testified in the holy Scriptures, he left his country, he left his friends, and after much patient suffering, finished his labors at Danbury, April 2, 1771, Æ 53 years.' (John Hayward, The Book of Religions [Boston, 1842] 396–7.)

21. The letter is dated August 29, 1867.

William White was the author of Emanuel Swedenborg: His Life and Writings (2 vols., London, 1867), a biographical and critical work of much literary skill and much independence. White, like James, deplored the ecclesiasticism of the 'New Church,' and read Swedenborg for himself. White corresponded with James (eight of his letters are in the collection at Widener); he quotes James in his book on Swedenborg; and at an appropriate place in his book, he pays tribute: 'As a rarity as an original and independent expositor of Swedenborg, the name of Mr Henry James must not be forgotten. Almost unknown in England, he is familiar to the bolder metaphysicians of New England. Scholarly, cultivated far beyond the measure of most who have dealt with Swedenborg, he is master of a voluble and vigourous style, which some critics call coarse; certainly he rejects no epithet or illustration however "improper" which he considers graphic. In common with Margaret Fuller [cf. *Literature and Art* (N. Y., 1852), 164], it is not as a seer of ghosts, but as a seer of truths, that Swedenborg interests him.' (*Swedenborg*, II, 653.)

22. For Faraday's and Henry's relations, cf. *A Memorial of Joseph Henry* (Washington, 1880), 64 and 506: 'There was sympathy between these men; and Henry loved to dwell on the hours that he and Bache had spent in Faraday's society.'

23. See *A Plain and Full Account of the Christian Practises Observed by the Church in St Martin's-le-Grand, London, and other Churches (commonly called Sandemanian) in Fellowship with Them* [By Samuel Pike], Boston, 1776; also Hayward, 126-7. There is a copy of Pike's book in the Boston Public Library.

24. Hayward, *op. cit.*, 126.

25. The Rev. James Hervey, Anglican of the Evangelical school, best known for his turgid *Meditations and Contemplations among the Tombs* (1746), was also author of three volumes of dialogues upon religious topics, *Theron and Aspasio* (1755). The theology of this popular work was attacked by Sandeman in his *Letters on Theron and Aspasio* (1757).

26. Cf. Wm. James, *A Pluralistic Universe*, 304-5.

27. *Letters on Theron and Aspasio* (N. Y., 1838), 43–4, 46, 48, 295–7.

28. *An Impartial Examination of Mr Robert Sandeman's Letters . . .* , Part II. By Samuel Langdon, D.D. (Boston, 1769), 1–2.

29. William James did not include his father's edition of the *Letters* and a brief treatise, *Remarks on the Apostolic Gospel* (1840) in the Bibliography appended to *Literary Remains of Henry James,* the list purporting to be of James' own 'published works': the *Letters* is an edition; and the *Remarks* must have been privately printed for limited circulation, since no copy is known to exist, either in the Library of Congress, or elsewhere. For the attribution of these two works to James, see the annotated bibliography which appeared shortly after his death (Jan. 13, 1883) in the Boston *Literary World,* XIV, 9–10. This bibliography, which is obviously the basis of that in Appleton's *Cyclopædia of American Biography* (ed. Wilson and Fiske [N. Y., 1887] III, 397–8), is unsigned, but presumably was either furnished or approved by William James.

For James' connection with Sandemanianism, see the obituary account in the Boston *Evening Transcript,* Dec. 20, 1882.

CHAPTER III

1. *General Catalogue of the Theological Seminary, Princeton, N. J. From 1812 to 1856.* The marriage was performed on July 28 by the Mayor of New York, Isaac L. Varian (Hastings, *William James of Albany,* 11).

2. *Notes of a Son and Brother,* 177–9.

The present Mr Henry James, in his *Letters of William James* (I, 9), regrets that her son Henry, 'who might

have done justice, as no one else could, to her good sense
and to the grace of her mind and character, could not
bring himself to include an adequate account of her in
the "Small Boy and Others." To a reader who ventured
to regret the omission, he replied sadly, "Oh! My dear
Boy—that memory is too sacred!" William James spoke
of her very seldom after her death, but then always with
a sort of tender reverence that he vouchsafed to no one
else.'

3. *Society the Redeemed Form of Man,* 43-4.
4. The letter is dated from 21 Washington Place, N. Y.,
   July 9, 1843.
5. The date at which James and Emerson first met is fixed
   by an entry in the latter's journal on March 18, 1842:
   'Home from New York, where I read six lectures on the
   Times [cf. *Nature. An Essay; and Lectures on the Times,*
   London, 1844]. . . . In New York I became acquainted
   with Henry James, . . . Horace Greeley, Albert Brisbane
   . . .' (*Journals,* VI, 163).
6. From James' lecture on Emerson, published posthu-
   mously in the *Atlantic Monthly,* Dec. 1904 (XCIV, 741).
7. James' letter is headed merely 'March. Thurs. Evening,'
   but the date (*cf.* note 5) must be 1842.
   The correspondence between James and Emerson, to
   the extent of thirty-four of the former's letters and thirty-
   two of the latter's, is preserved in the Widener Library.
   Extracts from James' share, inaccurately reproduced, find
   incorporation in *Notes of A Son and Brother* (181-6,
   194-8, 200-9). My quotations are transcribed from the
   originals.
   The references to James in Emerson's Journals are frequent, and the index is incomplete; but the following list,
   I believe, includes them all: VI, 163, 372; VII, 63, 103-4,
   109, 272, 280, 393-4; IX, 189, 190, 278, 297, 341, 519, 520,
   522, 568; X, 56, 65, 77. Emerson's comments on James'

philosophy (apropos of *Substance and Shadow*) are given at IX, 520 and 522; at IX, 189, Dr E. W. Emerson has a good note on James' attitude toward Emerson.

8. H. James, *A Small Boy and Others*, 8.
9. *Journals*, VIII, 109.
10. *Notes of a Son and Brother*, 204.
11. Letter dated May 11 (1843).
12. Letter dated Oct. 3, 1843.
13. An undated letter of 1842.
14. Letter dated July 21, 1843.
15. Letter dated May 6, 1843.
16. Letter dated July 21, 1843.
17. *Writings of Thoreau* (Boston, 1906), VI, 80.
18. Letter dated May 6, 1843.
19. Letter of Oct. 3, 1843.
20. 'Henry James, Sr.,' an interview reported in the Boston *Sunday Herald*, April 17, 1881. For another version of James' conversation with Alcott, see M. A. de W. Howe's *Memories of a Hostess*, 76.
21. From James' long letter to the Boston *Herald*, April 24, 1881, in criticism of the interviewer's report.
22. Letter of May 11, 1843.
23. *A Correspondence between John Sterling and Ralph Waldo Emerson*, (Boston, 1897), 76. The letter of introduction is printed on the following page.
24. *Correspondence of Carlyle and Emerson* (ed. C. E. Norton, 1884), II, 38.
25. *Ibid.*, II, 47.
26. *Letters of Thos. Carlyle to Mill, Sterling and Browning*, (N. Y., 1923), 272.
27. 'Henry James, Sr.,' Boston *Sunday Herald*, April 17, 1881.
28. *Substance and Shadow*, 322.
29. *Literary Remains*, 424–5.
30. *Ibid.*, 428–9.
31. *Ibid.*, 451.

CHAPTER IV

1. *Society the Redeemed Form of Man*, 43–5.
2. *Ibid.*, 46–8.
3. *Ibid.*, 49–50. The name of the lady we owe to *Notes of a Son and Brother* (173–4). Henry regretted not having witnessed the encounter: 'I felt how the *real* right thing for me would have been the hurrying drama of the original rush, the interview with the admirable Mrs Chichester, the sweet legend of his and my mother's charmed impression of whom had lingered with us. . . .'
4. *S. R. F. M.*, 51.
5. 'Passages from the *Œconomia Regni Animalis,* and *De Cultu et Amore Dei,* of Swedenborg. With original comments thereon. By the late Samuel Taylor Coleridge,' Heraud's *Monthly Magazine,* June, 1841 (V, 607–16). This article is followed (pp. 616–20) by 'A Letter to the Editor of the Monthly Magazine on Coleridge's Comments.'
6. For James' relations with Wilkinson, *cf.* Clement J. Wilkinson, *John James Garth Wilkinson* (London, 1911), especially pp. 41–2, 48–9, 50–1, 55–7, 88–9, 156–7, 182–5, 188ff., 202.
7. *Notes of a Son and Brother,* 158–9.
8. *The Secret of Swedenborg,* 211.
9. *S.R.F.M.,* 57–8.
10. *Ibid.,* 56; *S. S.,* 13–14.
11. *Cf.,* for instance, the pages on 'Swedenborg and his Followers' in *Literary Remains,* 368–86.
12. *S. R. F. M.,* 57, 67–8. James' last work, *Spiritual Creation,* printed in the *Literary Remains,* further charges Swedenborg with being 'too preternaturally serious to give his critical faculties fair play. He was unfortunately of a

most devout temperament of mental habit, inclining him to an over-indulgent estimate of the merely pious element in the church—that element of fake show or deceptive appearance which is usually denominated Pharisaism. To say all in a word, Swedenborg's intellect was singularly deficient in *humor*. . . .' The charge that Swedenborg's works lack æsthetic savor finds repetition: 'Thus it is, that whether I read of heaven and its orderly peaceful vicissitudes, or of hell and its insane delights, and feel the while my moral sense amply satisfied, I must say that to my æsthetic sense . . . the result is very much the same in either case, being always very dull and prosaic, with the poetical element very nearly eliminated.' (309, 311-2.)

13. *S. R. F. M.*, 68. Swedenborg's purpose 'was not to argue principles, but simply to state and illustrate them by facts of experience [*Heaven and Hell* bears the sub-title, *Ex Auditis et Visis*] and observation, leaving the reader to do the needful argumentation for himself according to the wants of his heart and the measure of his understanding. . . . Swedenborg was all simply a *seer,* and in no sense a dogmatist or "thinker"' (*S. S.*, 39–40).

14. A review of *The Secret of Swedenborg* in the *Nation*, IX, 436–7.

15. *Literary Remains*, 112.

16. Julia A. Kellogg, *Philosophy of Henry James* (N. Y., 1883), 5–6.

17. Carl Theophilus Odhner's *Annals of the New Church* (Bryn Athyn, 1904), 165. It includes Swedenborg's life and the history of Swedenborgianism both within and without the organization of the New Jerusalem Church up to the year 1850. The work was never completed, but it covers the movement in its most influential period with accuracy and acumen. A scholarly work, it is in-

valuable for its bibliographies both of Swedenborg and of the voluminous 'collateral literature.' Odhner is the authority upon whom I principally depend for historical statements concerning Swedenborgianism. Since the completion of my book, Mrs Marguerite Block's *The New Church in the New World* (Holt, 1932) has made its appearance. An able and fully documented study, this is now the general reader's best introduction to its subject.

For the beginnings of New Church organization in England and America, see Odhner, 111, 116, 118–20, 124, 131–2, 165–6, and Block, *The New Church*, 73–111.

James Glen lectured on Swedenborg in Philadelphia and Boston as early as 1784. In 1787 Francis Bailey printed at Philadelphia the first New Church work published in America, *A Summary View of the Heavenly Doctrines*. Two years later, Bailey published by subscription one volume of Swedenborg's *True Christian Religion;* among the subscribers were Benjamin Franklin and Robert Morris. The first New Church sermon in America was delivered by an Anglican clergyman, the Rev. James Wilmer, at Baltimore in 1792; shortly after, the first American New Church Society was organized at Baltimore.

18. John Hayward, *The Book of Religions* (Boston, 1842), 330. The figures 'five thousand' must include readers and students of Swedenborg and families of members as well as those formally enrolled as members of the ecclesiasticism. The Convention Journals report a very much smaller number.

19. Homeopathy and the New Church have been associated since 1825, when Dr Hans Gram, an earnest New-Churchman, introduced the new system into America. The well-known homeopathic pharmacists, Boericke and Tafel of Philadelphia and Otis Clapp of Boston, were New-

Churchmen. The attempts to explain the principles of homeopathy in the light of the New Church have been many. Mention may be made of the first, an essay by W. E. P. in *The New Churchman,* 1844; a discussion by Messrs De Charms, Holcombe and Payne on 'The Affinity of Homeopathy with the Doctrines of the New Church,' *The New Church Repository,* 1850; Dr Bergman, 'The Relationship between Homeopathy and the New-Church Doctrines,' *New-Church Review,* 1926; and J. E. Young, 'Homeopathy and Swedenborg's Teachings,' *ibid.,* 1924. *Philosophy in Homeopathy* (1890) is a little book by Charles S. Mack, Swedenborgian clergyman and homeopathic physician. On the general *'Intellectual Environment'* of the Swedenborgians, *cf.* Block, *The New Church,* 130–69.

20. Professor Clarence Hotson has done a painstaking and valuable Harvard dissertation on the influence of Swedenborg upon Emerson, many portions of which have been published. A series of four papers on 'Emerson and the Doctrine of Correspondence' appears in the *New-Church Review,* XXXVI, 47, 173, 304, 435; 'Emerson's Philosophical Sources for "Swedenborg" ' in *The New Philosophy,* XXXI, 482; 'Emerson's Title for "Swedenborg" [The Mystic]' in *New Church Life,* XLIX, 390.

    The principal answer to Emerson's lecture was Professor Bush's *Reply to Ralph Waldo Emerson on Swedenborg,* N. Y., 1846.

21. In his lecture, 'Swedenborg, the Mystic,' included in *Representative Men* (1850   ), Emerson wrote, Swedenborg 'has at last found a pupil in Dr Wilkinson, a philosophic critic, with a co-equal vigour of understanding and imagination comparable only to Lord Bacon's. . . . The admirable preliminary discourses with which Dr Wilkinson has enriched these volumes throw all the Contemporary Philosophy of England into the shade . . .'

22. Odhner's *Annals,* 512. In 1846, Bush published his influential apologia, *A Statement of Reasons for Embracing the Doctrines and Disclosures of Emanuel Swedenborg.*

23. In the preface to the revised edition of his book (Boston, 1861), Dr Pond tell us, 'When I entered upon the examination of Swedenborgianism, fourteen years ago, great efforts were being made by Prof. Bush and others [the Rev. B. F. Barrett lectured at Bangor, Dr Pond's own city, in 1846], to disseminate the doctrine, and give its currency with the people. Public lectures were delivered in our cities and villages, and select portions of the writings of Swedenborg, neatly printed and done up, and accompanied with prefatory and explanatory remarks were industriously circulated.'

24. Heraud's essay on Swedenborg appeared in the *Monthly Magazine,* May, 1841 (V, 441–72) as Chapter IV of 'Foreign Aids to Self-Intelligence,' a series of papers on the mystics.

25. *Literary Remains,* 112.

26. For the authoritative statement of Swedenborg's theology, *cf.* his *Vera Christiana Religio* (1st ed., 1771; an intelligent and useful compendium is Wm. F. Wunsch's *Gist of Swedenborg* (Philadelphia, 1920).

27. W. J. L. Sheppard puts the case very fairly in his *Swedenborgianism* (London, S. P. C. K., 1928), 3–4.

28. *Cf.* J. J. G. Wilkinson, *A Sketch of Swedenborg, and Swedenborgians* (Boston, 1842), 12–3, on the 'non-separatist Swedenborgians.'

29. 'Still, as I have said, I am not unwilling to admit that I do hold *ex animo* to the letter of Christian doctrine, and especially to the fact of central significance in it; the birth of Jesus Christ from the womb of a *virgin,* or *unmarried* woman." *New-Church Independent,* April, 1881, p. 161.

30. *New-Church Independent,* May 1881, p. 229.
31. *Ibid.,* p. 230.
32. *Christianity the Logic of Creation,* 2, 7, 6.
33. Clement Wilkinson, *J. J. G. Wilkinson,* 156, 157.
34. *New-Church Independent,* April 1881, p. 169.
35. *Lectures and Miscellanies,* 61.
36. *Ibid.,* 168.
37. 'All Religion has relation to Life, and the Life of Religion is to do Good' (Swedenborg, *Doctrine of Life for the New Jerusalem,* Chap. I).
38. *Substance and Shadow,* 237.
39. *S. R. F. M.,* 335, 350.
40. *Letter to a Swedenborgian,* 3.
41. *Ibid.,* 4.
42. *Ibid.,* 7–8.
43. *Ibid.,* 10.
44. *Ibid.,* 11–2.
45. *Ibid.,* 12. On page 14, there is another allusion to the Anglo-Catholics: 'Others are pilfering the Romish church of its festivals and fasts, to make them grotesque and contemptible by a purely wilful observance. . . .'
46. *Letter,* 15.
47. Odhner's *Annals,* 418, 428.
48. *Letter,* 18.
49. *Harbinger,* IV, 330.
50. *Letter,* 22.

CHAPTER V

1. *Harbinger,* II, 312–4 (April 25, 1846). James wrote the *Harbinger* a long letter in reply to this review, charging the Fourierists with attempting to 'restore the lost Paradise not by the true method of purifying the human

heart from its inordinate lusts . . . but by a direct appeal
to man's self-love.' (II, 378–9.)

2. *What Constitutes the State*, 5.
3. *Ibid.*, 17.
4. *Ibid.*, 15.
5. *Ibid.*, 17.
6. *Ibid.*, 20.
7. *Ibid.*, 21, 26.
8. *Ibid.*, 21, 22.
9. *Ibid.*, 24, 30.
10. *Ibid.*, 32.
11. *Ibid.*, 42–5.
12. Parke Godwin was a seminary mate of James at Princeton. Twenty-one of James' letters to Godwin of a much later date (1861–1882) are in the possession of the N. Y. Public Library.
13. Charles Fourier, *Oeuvres Complètes* (Paris, 1841), IV, 214.
14. Ch. Pellarin, *Life of Charles Fourier* (Tr. by F. G. Shaw, N. Y., (1848), 81.
15. *Cf.* Charles Gide's *Selections from the Works of Fourier* (London, 1901), 13–17, for examples of Fourier's fantasy.
16. For the Leroysville phalanx, see John Humphrey Noyes, *History of American Socialisms* (Philadelphia, 1870), 259–64. Dr Lemuel C. Belding, a clergyman of the New Jerusalem Church, was the active projector of the colony. For the Canton phalanx, see Odhner, *Annals*, 509, and Block, *The New Church*, 153–4. There was also a community, at Yellow Springs, Ohio, which combined the social views of Robert Owen with Swedenborgianism; see Noyes' *History*, 59–65.
17. Parke Godwin, *A Popular View of the Doctrines of Charles Fourier* (N. Y., 1844), 106. The arrangement and the substance of most of the chapters come from Renaud's *Vue Synthétique*.

18. Noyes, *History of American Socialisms,* Chapter XLI, 'Brook Farm and Swedenborgianism.' A useful account, for the most part trustworthy.

An essay on 'Fourier's Writings' (*Harbinger* I, 333–5) says of its subject that Plato, Goethe, and Swedenborg are 'the only minds with whom we can compare him for grandeur and breadth of conception.' Another essay (*ibid.,* I, 353–5), devoted to Swedenborg, puts him in the class with those 'great geniuses, Mesmer, Fourier, Hahnemann, Gall [phrenologist], Jacotot [educationalist; *floruit* 1830].'

19. C. Wilkinson, *J. J. G. Wilkinson,* 55. For an account of Doherty, cf. *Harbinger,* VII, 141.

20. *Ibid.,* 56. In the course of his essay in *Aesthetic Papers* (Boston, 1849), there are sundry allusions to Fourier,— *e.g.* (p. 134), 'the penetrating, celestial Swedenborg . . . the gigantic and earthborn Fourier. . . .'

21. The quotations come from a long review of Hempel in George Bush's *New Church Repository* (I, 540, 606) and a shorter review by Caleb Reed in the *New Jerusalem Magazine* (XXI, 299).

In the course of reviewing Hempel, Reed characterizes James' anonymously published *Letter to a Swedenborgian* as belonging to the same school of thought: attributing evil as well as good to God; teaching determinism.

22. *The True Organization of the New Church,* 13–4. For the authorship of the book, cf. a review in the Sept. and Oct. 1848 nos. of Bush's *Repository* and Odhner, *op. cit.,* 552.

23. *Harbinger,* VI, 132, 140 (the quotations were selected by James [cf. index to volume]; VII, 7 (notice by Ripley).

24. J. H. Noyes, *History of American Socialisms,* 200–32. M. Hillquit, *History of Socialism in the U. S.* (1910 edition), 79–83.

25. *Cf.* 'The Conversion of Brook Farm to Fourierism,' Chap. XXXIX in Noyes, *op. cit.* The prospectus of the *Harbinger* is reprinted in J. T. Codman's *Brook Farm* (1894), 101–3.

26. Noyes, 14–9; Hillquit, 87–108.

27. From an excellent essay on Fourier by Émile Faguet, *Politiques et Moralistes du Dix-Neuvième Siècle, 2ième série* (1898), 55–6.

28. Pellarin, *Life of Fourier*, 83–4. For an excellent summary of Fourier's theory of the passions in his own words, *cf.* Charles Gide's *Selections (op. cit.)*, 47–66.

29. Fourier, *Oeuvres Complètes*, V, 156–63.

30. Victor Hennequin, *Love in a Phalanstery* (N. Y., 1848), 18. This exposition of Fourier's views upon sex was translated by Henry James. Perhaps the best statement of the marriage series (*i.e.*, the *natural* and hence permissible degrees of latitude) is to be found on p. 12.

31. *Ibid.*, 5. Professor Larrabee writes: 'Of course the Saint-Simonians *also* got into bad odor from their later sex teachings, so that all French sects were suspicious.'

32. *Lectures and Miscellanies*, 48.

33. *Moralism and Christianity* (1st edition), 108–9. And cf. *Lectures*, 81–2.

34. *Lectures*, 84.

35. *Ibid.*, 85, 87.

36. *Moralism and Christianity*, 126.

37. *Ibid.*, 29.

38. *Ibid.*, 33, 32.

39. *Harbinger*, VIII, 101. (July 29, 1848.)

40. *Ibid.*, VIII, 53.

41. *Ibid.*, VIII, 37; VII, 197–8.

42. For James' authorship of this translation, *cf.* the *Harbinger*, VII, 197, 'The Observer and Hennequin' (assigned to James in the index prefaced to vol. VII).

43. *Cf.* the *Harbinger*, VII, 197, and the controversy in Vol.

VIII between 'A. E. F.' and 'Y. S.' (Henry James): 12-3; 36-7; 44-5; 53-4; 60-1; 68-9.

Clarence Gohdes, who gives, in his *Periodicals of American Transcendentalism* (Durham, N. C., 1931) an interesting account of the *Harbinger*, speaks of James as having 'precipitated a controversy between the liberals and the conservatives among its Swedenborgian readers,' but seems unaware that James was one of those readers whom he mentions as 'airing their views about the charges made against Fourier's notions of sexual morality,' with the consequence that the *Harbinger* 'ended its days in the midst of miserable wrangling' (Gohdes, 130-1).

'A. E. F.' (The Rev. Alfred E. Ford), once an Episcopal clergyman of Aiken, S. C., became a New-Churchman in 1846; was re-ordained in 1847; served as pastor of the Delaware County Society 1847-50 and of the N. Y. Society, 1853-5. His translation of Werner's *Guardian Spirits* was published in 1847.

44. Dr Lazarus was also the author of *The Human Trinity, Passional Hygiene and Natural Medicine,* and *Vegetable Portraits of Character* (analogies and 'correspondences'; largely translation from Fourier).

45. For Andrews, *cf.* the new *Dictionary of American Biography*, I, 298.

46. *Love, Marriage, and Divorce*, 38.

47. *Ibid.*, 74-6.

48. Apparently with the removal of the *Harbinger* to N. Y. in November, James began backing the paper financially, for Garth Wilkinson writes him, Dec. 18, 1847: 'Glad your spare cash goes into the *Harbinger*.'

49. *Spiritual Wives* (London, 1868), 391.

50. *Secret of Swedenborg*, 241. The 'Postscript' to the *Secret* is a spirited reply to Dixon, who 'manages, indeed, in the brief paragraph he devotes to me to tell as many untruths, very nearly, as there are words in the paragraph.'

51. 'Henry James, Sr.,' Boston *Sunday Herald*, April 17, 1881.
52. James' contributions are signed 'Y. S.'
53. *Notes of a Son*, 193–4.
54. *Harbinger*, VII, 150. The review of James' *Last of the Fairies* appeared in Vol. VI, 111.
55. *Spirit of the Age*, I, 49–51 ('Vanity Fair, or Becky Sharp'); 113 (Blake).
56. *Harbinger*, VI, 15. Advertised also on pp. 32 and 40 of the same volume.
57. Prominently featured in the early volumes of the *Harbinger* were Francis G. Shaw's translations of George Sand's *Consuelo* and the *Countess of Rudolstadt*.
58. *Spirit of the Age*, I, 265.
59. *Ibid.*, II, 152–5; 168–71.
60. According to the announcement in the *Harbinger*, the *New Times* was to commence publication in Jan. 1848.
61. *Harbinger*, VI, 37.
62. E. W. Emerson, *Early Years of the Saturday Club*, 325.
63. 'This play of his remarkable genius brought him in fact throughout the long years no ghost of a reward in the form of pence, and could proceed to publicity, as it repeatedly did, not only by the copious and resigned sacrifices of such calculations, but by his meeting in every single case all the expenses of the process.' (*Notes of a Son*, 155.)
64. *Moralism and Christianity*, 41.
65. *Ibid.*, 61–2.
66. *Ibid.*, 63–4.
67. *Ibid.*, 80.
68. *Ibid.*, 67–8, 81.
69. James' letters to the N. Y. *Tribune* are said to have attracted much attention. The first, under the heading, 'An American in Europe,' appeared in the issue of Sept. 3, 1855; the fourteenth and last on Sept. 11, 1856. Some of

the matter of these letters was incorporated in the second, enlarged edition of the *Church of Christ*.

70. Letter III, dated 24 Aug. 1855; *The Church of Christ* (2nd ed.), 95–6.

71. Letter III; *C. of C.*, 98–9.

72. Letter IV; *C. of C.*, 101, 104–5.

73. As late as 1868, some allusions to Fourier in Emerson's lecture on Brook Farm aroused James to protest. The *Commonwealth*, Nov. 28, 1868, reports James 'very mad about Emerson's criticism on Fourier; he says Emerson knows nothing about Fourier, and has confessed to him that he never read his works, but only knows of them through extracts . . .' James replied (Dec. 5, 1868 issue): 'I am not specially retained by the fates to defend Fourier whenever his reputation is assailed, but . . . I am free to say that Mr Emerson did not, in my opinion, do justice to Fourier. . . .' *Cf.* also James' letter in the issue of Dec. 12, 'Mr James further concerning Emerson, Fourier, and "Warrington." Fourier's System Explained.'

74. *Literary Remains*, 27.

75. *Ibid.*, 26.

76. *Love, Marriage, and Divorce* (1853 ed.), 10–12.

77. *Notes of a Son*, 210.

CHAPTER VI

1. *A Small Boy and Others*, (N. Y., 1913), 48–9.

2. *Notes of a Son*, 68–70.

3. *Society the Redeemed Form of Man*, 42.

4. *Ibid.*, 88.

5. *A Small Boy*, 232–4.
6. *Notes of a Son*, 170, 169, 164.
7. *Ibid.*, 167.
8. *A Small Boy*, 216.
9. *Ibid.*, 16.
10. *Notes of a Son*, 195–6.
11. *Cf.* James' first two letters to the N. Y. *Tribune*, in which he describes the Geneva schools.
12. *A Small Boy*, 312.
13. *Ibid.*, 324–8.
14. *Ibid.*, 363–9.
15. *Ibid.*, 396–419.
16. *Notes of a Son*, 2–4.
17. *Ibid.*, 7–12.
18. *Ibid.*, 28.
19. *Ibid.*, 50–1; 61–2. *Letters of Wm. James*, I, 23–4.
20. *Notes of a Son*, 304; 67.
21. *Ibid.*, 82.
22. *Letters of Henry James* (ed. P. Lubbock), I, 6–9.
23. *Early Years of the Saturday Club* (ed. E. W. Emerson), 328.
24. *Notes of a Son*, 109–10.
25. *Ibid.*, 111–2.
26. *Ibid.*, 112–5.
27. M. E. Sargent, *Sketches and Reminiscences of the Radical Club* (1880), 38.
28. *Letters of Henry James*, I, 10.
29. *Notes of a Son*, 52.
30. *A Small Boy*, 214–5.
31. *Notes of a Son*, 169, 171.
32. *Ibid.*, 229, 228.
33. *Letters of Henry James*, I, 111.
34. Mrs Orr, 'Mr Henry James, Sr.', *Athenaeum*, July 24, 1880. Foster Damon (*Chivers* [N. Y., 1930], 21) writes fancifully: 'Perhaps the step from Swedenborg to the

society novels of Henry James, Jr. may seem surprising. Yet, given the Swedenborgian habit of mind, and developing it in the social world, you have his novels.'

35. *Letters of Wm. James,* I, 20, 119–20.
36. *Ibid.,* 21–2.
37. *Notes of a Son,* 51.
38. 'Swedenborg's Ontology,' *North American Review,* July 1867.
39. *Letters of Wm. James,* I, 96–7.
40. Letter dated Sept. 27, 1867.
41. *Letters of Wm. James,* I, 169–70.
42. *Ibid.,* 220.
43. J. S. Bixler, *Religion in the Philosophy of Wm. James* (1926), 159.
44. *Letters of Wm. James,* I, 241–2.

Morris R. Cohen has said of William James himself what William in substance said of his father: 'His thoughts ran in vivid pictures, and he could not trust logical demonstration as much as his intuitive suggestions.' Hence he was never an effective answerer to the criticisms of dialecticians like Royce, Bradley, and Bertrand Russell.

45. Wm. James, *A Pluralistic Universe,* 20–1.
46. *Letters of W. James,* I, 219.
47. Woodbridge Riley, *American Thought* (N. Y., 1915), 329, 338.
48. *Literary Remains,* 118.
49. *Cf.* Chapter VIII, 'The Philosophy,' pp. 192–5.
50. These two sayings were reported to me by my friend, the Rev. L. F. Hite, Professor of Philosophy in the New Church Theological School, Cambridge, who was for a number of years a student in William James' seminars.
51. Bixler, *Religion in the Phil. of W. J.,* 197. Reported to Bixler by George Herbert Palmer.
52. *Letters of W. J.,* I, 310.

53. *Character and Opinion in the U. S.* (1920), 66. *Cf.* also p. 10.
54. *Cf.*, for example, R. B. Perry's in *Present Philosophical Tendencies* ('The Philosophy of Wm. James'), especially pp. 376–8.

CHAPTER VII

1. *Notes of a Son and Brother*, 61.
2. The *Tribune* letters appeared in the issues of Sept. 3, 8, and 22, Jan. 15 and 16, Feb. 7, March 17, August 26, Sept. 12 and 16, and Oct. 1, 1856. I am indebted for the loan of a photostatic transcription of these letters to S. C. Eby, Esq., of N. Y., who proposes to bring out an edition of them.
3. Letter 9; *Church of Christ* (2nd ed.), 108.
4. Letter 10.
5. *The Social Significance* (1861), 13.
6. *Ibid.*, 14–5.
7. *Ibid.*, 9.
8. *Notes of a Son*, 62.
9. *Ibid.*, 155.
10. *Ibid.*, 227.
11. *Ibid.*, 155.
12. Review of *The Nature of Evil* by Jas. Freeman Clarke, *Christian Examiner*, LIX, 116–36. Review of *The Secret of Swedenborg* by C. S. Peirce, *North American Review*, CX, 463–8. Review of *Society the Redeemed Form of Man*, by George H. Howison, *Christian Register*, July 12, 1879. *Cf.* James' reply, *C. R.*, July 26; Howison's reply, August 16; James' reply to Howison's reply, August

30. 'Mr. Henry James, Senior' (a really brilliant essay
in review of *S. R. F. M.*), by A[lexandra] Orr [Mrs
Sutherland Orr, author of the *Browning Handbook* and
the *Life and Letters of Browning*. Cf. *Letters of Henry
James*, I, 112], London *Athenaeum*, July 24, 1880.
13. *Literary Remains*, 11–2.

Besides Miss Kellogg, James had an able disciple and
expositor in the Rev. Charles H. Mann, the liberal pastor
of the New-Church Society in Orange, N. J., and for
some years editor of the *New Church Messenger*. Mann
brought out, in 1906, an edition of James' *Morality and
the Perfect Life*, and, apparently about the same time,
a brochure of his own, *God in Man and How to Worship
Him There*, of particular interest as showing one very
logical interpretation of the Jamesian theology. 'God is
ESSENTIAL MAN. He is the Reality in man. It is
because of His presence within that man is man. Thus
this teaching means that God is in human nature: and
that He is in each individual according to his possession
of human nature' (p. 5).

Samuel C. Eby never knew James in the flesh, but he
has been an almost life-long exponent of the Jamesian
philosophy and a diligent bibliographer of Jamesiana.
Mr Eby was formerly a New-Church clergyman and
served for a time as editor of the *Messenger*. He has published a very intelligent and well-written little book,
Swedenborg's Service to Philosophy (Peoria, Ill., 1891),
which interprets Swedenborg after the fashion of Henry
James. Eby's book and the Rev. L. F. Hite's paper,
'Ultimate Reality' (*Transactions of the International Swedenborg Congress*, London, 1910), are the two most
philosophically competent accounts of Swedenborg we
have.

The letters of William White convey news of a little
group of English Jamesians. White, whose *Swedenborg*

James pronounced 'almost a model in its kind, and [one which] does emphatic credit both to his intellect and his conscience' [*Secret of Swedenborg*, 12], twice refers to his design for a small volume of selections from James' writings. Edward Welch, an architect, was meditating a similar volume. Horace Field, author of *Union with God*, deeply admired James; some of his letters, along with White's, are at Widener. White writes (Jan. 12, 1868): '*Certes* you take hold of people! I was hearing of Mr Down, a dyer in the Strand, who keeps one or other of your books always in his pocket.'

The 'little clan' of ardent Jamesians has never died out, as my correspondence of the last six years can testify. *Cf.* Alice Spiers Sechrist's 'Henry James the Elder' in the *New-Church Messenger*, Sept. 3, 1930 and a striking letter written by S. Marshall Ilsley to the *New Republic* (August 22, 1928).

14. Julia A. Kellogg (1830–1914) taught school in Brooklyn for some years. Later, living with friends in Cambridge, she became acquainted with the elder Henry James, 'whose expositions of Swedenborg's philosophy [Miss Kellogg, reared a Presbyterian, had already passed through Unitarianism to an interest in Swedenborg] she accepted as eminently and entirely satifying. It is said [and I should suppose the saying quite true] that Mr James regarded her as the one among his disciples who most fully grasped his views.'

In her old age, Miss Kellogg lived at Orange, N. J., with her friend, Miss Charlotte Schetter, to whom she bequeathed her large collection of letters written her by Mr James. Soon after the publication of *Progress and Poverty*, Miss Kellogg became an ardent follower of Henry George; and to the cause of single tax she thereafter gave persistent devotion. At eighty, she published an abridgement of P. E. Dove's *Theory of Human Pro-*

gression, a book which gave much satisfaction to Georgians. ('Julia A. Kellogg,' by Alice Thacher Post, *The Public* [Chicago], XVIII, 79–80.)

15. *New-Church Independent,* XXXI (1883), 48.
16. *Early Years of the Saturday Club* (ed. E. W. Emerson), 322–5.
17. *Notes of a Son,* 211.
18. Sanborn, *Recollections of Seventy Years,* II, 383–5; and *cf.* Sanborn and Harris, *A. Bronson Alcott,* I, 276–7, and Thoreau, *Writings* (Boston, 1906), VI, 345.
19. M. A. De Wolfe Howe, *Memories of a Hostess* (Boston, 1922), 72.
20. *Ibid.,* 79, 83.
21. *Ibid.,* 72–3, 75.
22. The *Commonwealth,* Sept. 12, 1868. M. A. Howe, *Memories of a Hostess,* 79–80. Julia Ward Howe, *Reminiscences,* 324 (*cf. ibid.,* 323–6).
23. 'Henry James, Sr.,' Boston *Sunday Herald,* April 17, 1881; Boston *Evening Transcript,* Dec. 20, 1882; N. Y. *Nation,* Dec. 22, 1882.
24. 'Mr Henry James Explains Certain Statements Recently Published,' *Herald,* April 24, 1881.
25. In a letter to Emerson, dated Jan. 18, 1865, James writes that he is 'lecturing tomorrow on Carlyle. Drew parallel between him and you—sending you the lecture.' Under the date of Feb. 13, 1872, he reports to Emerson that the Mrs Fields had asked him to read a paper on R. W. E. at her *salon,* and announces his desire that Mrs Emerson, Ellen, Elizabeth Hoar, and Elizabeth Ripley should be among the audience.

The Carlyle lecture of 1865 may in part have been what appeared in the just established *Nation* (I, 20–1) apropos of Vols. 5 and 6 of Carlyle's *Frederick the Great.* For its attribution to James, cf. *A General Index to the Nation* (Boston, 1880).

26. *Literary Remains,* 423, 459, 445. These quotations come from James' 'Some Personal Recollections of Thomas Carlyle,' first published, after Carlyle's death, in the *Atlantic,* May, 1881. James is in part quoting from his journal.
27. *Ibid.,* 433–4, 445.
28. Howe, *Memories of a Hostess,* 79.
29. F. L. Mott, 'Carlyle's American Public,' *Philological Q.,* IV, 245–64.
30. *Cf.* note 25.
31. *Atlantic Monthly,* XCIV, 742–4.
   The *Atlantic* version of the lecture, published in 1904 with an introduction by William James, is a much contracted one. Manuscripts of two different texts, both voluminous, survive at Widener. In both James persistently digresses from Emerson to mount his own hobbies.
32. *Atlantic,* XCIV, 740.
33. *Literary Remains,* 293, 294 ('Mr Emerson,' Chap. X; cf. *Spiritual Creation*).
34. *Ibid.,* 301–2.
35. For all its characteristic extravagance, James expressed himself sincerely enough when he wrote Emerson in 1849: 'There is nothing I dread so much as literary men, especially *our* literary men; catch them out of range of mere personal gossip about authors and books and ask them for honest sympathy in your sentiment, or for an honest repugnancy of it, and you will find the company of stage-drivers sweeter and more comforting to your soul. In truth the questions which are beginning to fill the best books, and will fill the best for a long time to come, are not related to what we have called literature, and are as well judged—I think better—by those whom books have at all events not belittled.' *Notes of a Son,* 194.
36. *Ibid.,* 207–9.
37. Letter to the Boston *Herald* of April 24, 1881.

38. *Literary Remains*, 75.
39. From an unpublished letter.
40. Ogden, *Life and Letters of E. L. Godkin*, II, 117.
41. *Society the Redeemed Form of Man*, 89–90.
42. *Literary Remains*, 7–8, 10.
43. Unpublished letter in N. Y. Public Library.
44. *Letters of Henry James*, I, 97–8.
45. *Letters of Wm. James*, I, 16.
46. 'In Memory of Henry James,' *New Church Independent*, XXXI (Feb. 1883), 88–9.

CHAPTER VIII

1. William James, in *Literary Remains*, 9–10.
2. *Cf.* especially *Letter to a Swedenborgian* (1847) and *The Church of Christ not an Ecclesiasticism* (1854).
3. Henry James, *Society the Redeemed Form of Man*, 480.
4. *Cf.*, e.g., F. L. Pattee, *Hist. of Am. Lit. since 1810*, (N. Y., 1915), 187.
5. *Society the Redeemed Form of Man*, 31, 34, 33–4.
6. *Secret of Swedenborg*, 21; *Society the Redeemed Form of Man*, 58.
7. *Society the Redeemed Form of Man*, 114.
8. *Secret of Swedenborg*, 129, 70, 35.
9. *Ibid.*, 36–7.
10. *Sapientia Angelica de Divino Amore et de Divina Sapientia* (1763), Part I, sections 47–9.
11. *Secret of Swedenborg*, 90.
12. *Ibid.*, 139.
13. *Ibid.*, 186.
14. *Ibid.*, 169.

15. *Society the Redeemed Form of Man*, 169–70.
16. *Ibid.*, 386.
17. *Ibid.*, 388; *Secret of Swedenborg*, 162.
18. *Secret of Swedenborg*, 221.
19. *Christianity the Logic of Creation*, 66.
20. *Secret of Swedenborg*, 161.
21. *Ibid.*, 221.
22. *Ibid.*, 81.
23. *Ibid.*, 223.
24. *Lectures and Miscellanies* (N. Y., 1852), 196–200.
25. *Christianity the Logic of Creation*, 12.
26. *Literary Remains*, 15.
27. *Ibid.*, 366.
28. *Society the Redeemed Form of Man*, 13.
29. *Literary Remains*, 13. Julia A. Kellogg, *The Philosophy of Henry James: A Digest*, 4–5.
30. *Literary Remains*, 113.
31. *Cf.* Clement J. Webb, *God and Personality*, 62–3, 84–5.
32. *Literary Remains*, 209; *Lectures and Miscellanies*, 147; *Society the Redeemed Form of Man*, 331–3.
33. *Sapientia Angelica*, Part I, sec. 11.
34. *Society the Redeemed Form of Man*, 264.
35. *Literary Remains*, 365, 363.
36. *The Church of Christ not an Ecclesiasticism* (2nd edition, London, 1856), 104–5.
37. *Literary Remains*, 15.
38. *Ibid.*, 362.
39. *Ibid.*, 353.
40. *Ibid.*, 106–7.
41. This is once intimated by William James (*Letters*, I, 241): 'The world of his thought had a *few elements*. . . . *Those* elements were very deep ones, and had theological names.'
42. *Society the Redeemed Form of Man*, 15, 13.

BIBLIOGRAPHY

A. Books by the elder Henry James.

1. Robert Sandeman's *Letters on Theron and Aspasio.* New York: John S. Taylor 1838, pp. xx, 500 [Edited with two pages of unsigned preface by James].
2. [*Remarks on the Apostolic Gospel,* 1840.]
3. *What Constitutes the State.* N. Y.: John Allen, 1846. Pp. 59.
4. *Tracts for the New Times. No. I. Letter to a Swedenborgian.* N. Y.: John Allen, 1847, pp. 24 [Nos. II and III were by J. J. G. Wilkinson].
5. Victor Hennequin's *Love in a Phalanstery.* N. Y.: Dewitt and Davenport, 1848, pp. 27 [Translated from the French (*Les Amours au Phalanstère,* Paris, 1847) and with a two page unsigned preface by James].
6. *Moralism and Christianity; Or, Man's Experience and Destiny.* In three Lectures. New York: Redfield, 1850, pp. 184. Second edition, 1850, pp. 53. [Consists of three lectures, 'A Scientific Statement of the Christian Doctrine of the Lord, or Divine Man,' 'Socialism and Civilization in Relation to the Development of the Individual Life,' and 'Morality and the Perfect Life.' The third essay, 'Morality and the Perfect Life', was reprinted,

with some omissions and alterations, by the New
Church Educational Association, Elkhart, Indiana,
1906, with an 'Introductory Word' by Charles H.
Mann.]

7. *Lectures and Miscellanies.* N. Y.: Redfield 1852, pp.
442. [Contains six 'lectures,' 'Democracy and its Issues,'
'Property as a Symbol,' 'The Principle of Universality
in Art,' 'The Old and New Theology,' Parts I and II
(*cf.* no. 11) and 'The Scientific Accord of Natural
and Revealed Religion,' and ten 'miscellanies,' 'The
Laws of Creation,' 'Berkeley and his Critics,' 'God,'
'Man,' 'Responsibility,' 'Morality,' 'A Very Long Letter,'
'Spiritual Rappings,' 'Intemperance,' and 'Christianity.']

8. *Love, Marriage and Divorce, A Discussion between
Henry James, Horace Greeley, and Stephen Pearl An-
drews.* N. Y.: Stringer and Townsend, 1853, pp. 103.
*Love, Marriage and Divorce, A Discussion between
Henry James, Horace Greeley, and Stephen Pearl
Andrews. Including the final replies of Mr Andrews,
rejected by the New York Tribune, and a subsequent
discussion, occurring twenty years later, between Mr
James and Mr Andrews.* Boston, Mass.; Benj. R.
Tucker, Publisher, 1889.

9. *The Nature of Evil, considered in a letter to the Rev.
Edward Beecher, D.D. author of 'The Conflict of
Ages.'* New York: Appleton, 1855, pp. 348.

10. *The Church of Christ not an Ecclesiasticism: A Letter
of Remonstrance to a member of the* soi-disant *New
Church,* N. Y., Redfield 1854, pp. 72. Second edition,
London, W. White, 1856, pp. 156. [The second edition,
we are told in the preface, dated at London, includes
'considerable additions and some verbal alterations.'
The additions were drawn from the letters contributed,
1855-6, to the N. Y. *Daily Tribune.*]

11. *Christianity the Logic of Creation*. London, Wm. White, 1857, pp. 264. (N. Y., Appleton, 1857.)
12. *The Old and New Theology*
    London, Longman, Green, Longman and Roberts, 1861, pp. 197 [This is an English reprint of the two lectures, 'The Old and New Theology,' from *Lectures and Miscellanies*, together with *The Church of Christ not an Ecclesiasticism*, in the shorter form of the first (American) edition. The anonymous introduction is written from the Anglican 'Broad Church' point of view, probably by some disciple of Maurice].
13. *The Social Significance of our Institutions: An Oration delivered by request of the citizens at Newport, R. I., July 4, 1861.* Boston: Ticknor and Fields, 1861, pp. 47.
14. *Substance and Shadow; or, Morality and Religion in Their Relation to Life: An Essay on the Physics of Creation,* Boston: Ticknor and Fields, 1863, pp. 539. Second Edition Revised, 1866.
15. *The Secret of Swedenborg: Being an Elucidation of his Doctrine of the Divine Natural Humanity.* Boston: Fields, Osgood & Co., 1869, pp. xv, 243.
16. *Society the Redeemed Form of Man, and the Earnest of God's Omnipotence in Human Nature: Affirmed in Letters to a Friend.* Boston: Houghton, Osgood, & Co., 1879, pp. 485.
17. *The Literary Remains of the Late Henry James:* Edited with an introduction by William James. Boston: Houghton Mifflin Co., 1884, pp. 471.

B. Selections from James' magazine articles and reviews.

1. 'Swedenborg as a Theologian,' *Massachusetts Quarterly Review*, I (1848), 293-307.
2. 'Vanity Fair, or Becky Sharp,' *The Spirit of the Age*, I (1850), 49-51. (For Thackeray and James, *cf.* Eyre

Crowe, *With Thackeray in America* (1893), 43–4 and 167, and *A Small Boy*, 87–91.

3. Review of William Blake's Poems, *The Spirit of the Age*, I (1850), 113.

4. 'The Divine Man,' *Massachusetts Quarterly Review*, III (1850), 52–67.

5. 'The Works of Sir William Hamilton,' *Putnam's Magazine*, Nov. 1853.

6. Review of Carlyle's *Frederick the Great, Nation*, I (1865), 20–1.

7. 'Faith and Science,' *North American Review*, CI (1865), 335–78.

8. 'Stirling's *Secret of Hegel*,' *North American Review*, CII (1866), 264–75.

9. 'Is Marriage Holy?,'*Atlantic Monthly*, XXV (1870), 360–8.

10. 'Spiritualism, Old and New,' *Atlantic Monthly*, XXIX (1872), 358–62.

11. 'Personal Reminiscences of Carlyle,' *Atlantic Monthly*, XLVII (1881) 593–609.

12. 'Emerson,' *Atlantic Monthly*, XCIV (1904), 740–5.

C. Some of the more important books and articles concerning the life and philosophy of James.

1. Howells, William Dean. Review of *The Secret of Swedenborg, Atlantic Monthly*, XXIV (1869), 762–3.

2. Peirce, C. S. Review of *The Secret of Swedenborg, North American Review*, CX (1870), 463–8.

3. Orr, A. [Mrs Sutherland], 'Mr Henry James, Senior,' *The Athenaeum*, (1880).

4. 'Henry James, Senior' (Bibliography and tributes), *The Literary World*, XIV, (1883), 9–10.

5. Kellogg, J[ulia] A. *The Philosophy of Henry James*, Boston, 1883.

6. James, William. Introduction to *Literary Remains of the late Henry James,* (1884), 7–119.

7. Lackland, C. E. 'Henry James, the Seer,' *Journal of Speculative Philosophy,* XIX (1885), 53ff.

8. James, Henry, *A Small Boy and Others,* 1913.

9. James, Henry. *Notes of a Son and Brother,* 1914.

10. Emerson, E. W. 'Henry James,' *The Early Years of the Saturday Club* (1918), 322–33.

11. Hastings, Katherine B. *William James of Albany, N. Y. (1771–1832) and his Descendants.* . . . Reprinted from the *New York Genealogical and Biographical Record,* Vol. LV, 1924.

12. Larrabee, Harold A. 'Henry James, Sr., '30 at Union,' *Union Alumni Monthly,* XV (1926), 236–47.

13. Baugh, Hansell, 'Emerson and the Elder Henry James,' *The Bookman,* LXVIII (1928), 320–2.

14. Sechrist, Alice Spiers, 'Henry James the Elder,' *New-Church Messenger,* Sept. 3, 1930, pp. 203–6.

15. Larrabee, Harold A. 'The Jameses: Financier, Heretic, Philosopher,' *The American Scholar,* I (1932), 401–13.

16. Perry, Ralph Barton. 'Religion versus Morality according to the Elder Henry James,' *International Journal of Ethics,* XLII (1932), 289–303.

17. Warren, Austin. 'James and his Secret,' *Saturday Review of Literature,* VIII (1932), 759.

18. Grattan, C. Hartley. *The Three Jameses,* (N. Y., 1932), 21–107. *Cf.* my review in *American Literature,* V (1933), 176–9.

INDEX